As an African American, I am delighted with the publication of this book. It will serve as an excellent introduction to Reformed theology for the emerging black Reformed community in the United States. I anticipate that it will be a great resource for church planters and anyone else seeking to reach the black community.

—**Anthony B. Bradley,** Associate Professor of Theology and Ethics, The King's College; Author, *Liberating Black Theology: The Bible and Black Experience in America*

A most edifying and important work. I suspect that generations to come will look back upon its publication as a milestone in the history of the Reformed theology. This book needed to be written, and, more importantly, it needs to be read.

—**Keith A. Mathison,** Professor of Systematic Theology, Reformation Bible College

When I met Anthony Carter several years ago, I detected a rigorous mind, a righteous concern for racial justice, and a Reformed vision of God—a rare combination. Since then I have wanted to be a listener. Now this book makes that easier. May the Lord of nations use it to shape a powerful movement of God-centered Christians from all peoples who have tasted suffering.

—**John Piper,** Founder and Teacher, desiringGod.org; Chancellor, Bethlehem College and Seminary, Minneapolis

This work is greatly needed in the church, and I am confident the Lord will use it for the re-Africanization of the church.

—**Richard L. Pratt Jr.,** President, Third Millennium Ministries

BLACK&
REFORMED

BLACK&
REFORMED

SEEING GOD'S SOVEREIGNTY IN THE
AFRICAN-AMERICAN CHRISTIAN EXPERIENCE

Second Edition

ANTHONY J. CARTER

P&R
PUBLISHING
P.O. BOX 817 • PHILLIPSBURG • NEW JERSEY 08865-0817

Unless otherwise indicated, Scripture quotations are from The Holy Bible, New King James Version. Copyright © 1979, 1980, 1982, Thomas Nelson, Inc.

Printed in the United States of America

Library of Congress Cataloging-in-Publication Data

Names: Carter, Anthony J., 1967- author.
Title: Black and reformed : seeing God's sovereignty in the African-American Christian experience / Anthony J. Carter.
Other titles: On being black and reformed
Description: Second edition. | Phillipsburg : P&R Publishing, 2016. | Includes bibliographical references.
Identifiers: LCCN 2015043783| ISBN 9781629952307 (pbk.) | ISBN 9781629952314 (epub) | ISBN 9781629952321 (mobi)
Subjects: LCSH: Black theology. | African Americans--Religion. | Reformed Church--Doctrines.
Classification: LCC BT82.7 .C37 2016 | DDC 284/.208996073--dc23
LC record available at http://lccn.loc.gov/2015043783

To Adie

While I'm on this pilgrim journey,
I'm glad you hold my hand.

Contents

CONTENTS

Foreword

To be *black and* is a curious thing. This *"and"-ness* reflects a two-ness, a double consciousness made famous by sociologist W. E. B. DuBois.

It's an *and* with ambivalence. Sometimes the *and* does what *con*junctions are meant to do—it *joins* two objects or adjectives in a peaceful coexistence. But in the African-American experience, *and* sometimes signifies *dis*junctions—a series of impossibilities or at least improbabilities. In those instances, *and* reads like *but*. When he's described as "black *and* intelligent," the speaker implicitly denies black native intelligence. When she's described as "black *and* beautiful," the speaker suggests that beauty is a thing foreign to blackness. In such cases, the *and* reveals a speaker's difficulty putting the *black* together with a positive adjective, the way matching poles of two magnets refuse touching against their magnetic wills.

To be *black and* _____ isn't as simple as filling in the blank. There's a tension that must be addressed.

So much of African-American life is lived in that tension, in that in-between world populated by *ands* that so often negate *black*. I suspect this tension arises out of the centuries-long battle to define what it means to be black. A long line of assailants has attempted to make *black* an utterly negative thing, demeaning and defaming it. Placing beyond its reach those things belonging to other supposedly more noble creatures. So to be black meant *not* thinking white, *not* speaking white, *not* acting white, *not* owning what whites owned, *not* going where whites went, *not* being white. It was their *not* that gave an incredulous tone to the *and* in the phrase *black and* ____.

So in cultural, legal, and psychological self-defense, a long line of African Americans redefined what it means to be black, dignifying and beautifying blackness over and against its despisers. They sang with James Brown, "Say it loud—I'm black *and* I'm proud." They made beauty products called Black & Beautiful. They celebrated being "young, gifted *and* black." What the popular imagination separated, these artists, activists, and everyday folks reappropriated. They restored the conjunction to its proper use and restored to *black* a positive potential.

But all that happened largely in the world of art, culture, and politics. It was long past time that someone did in theological circles what Tony Carter did in *On Being Black and Reformed*—unabashedly break the back of that two-ness, that *and-ness* that said you couldn't really be black *and* Reformed.

This book, in God's providence, came along at a time when African-American Christians of conservative biblical faith needed to be assured that to be Christian—specifically a Reformed Christian—was not a contradiction to being black. In God's kindness, the book came along when people in search of a spiritual identity greater than *black* and greater than *Reformed* were listening. What they heard in *On Being Black and Reformed* was a clarion call to be so deeply Christian that all the Christian tradition could belong to all Christ's people *as Christian people*—black, white, Asian, Latin and Hispanic, Reformed and not. What they heard—perhaps for the first time in African-American Christian writing—was a brother and friend telling them in love that the *and* was not a tension but an invitation. An invitation to embrace what some said couldn't be embraced and to find in that embrace more of Christ and his wondrous love.

I remember when I was first introduced to *On Being Black and Reformed*. It was at a small dinner made up mostly of black and Reformed pastors. We were getting to know each other with that sheepish caution and wonder that comes when you discover you're not the only one. We asked questions of each other and listened, making sure the theological and the cultural shibboleths were accurately pronounced. Then one brother asked me, "Have you read Tony Carter's *On Being Black and Reformed?*" I confessed that I had not, and with that confession he slowly leaned back in his chair, satisfied that he was both more black and more Reformed than me. The next day I picked up a copy of the book and began to devour it.

To my delight, I discovered that day that not only was I not alone but that the Lord had raised up a witness who was intelligent, articulate, passionate, discerning, courageous, black, and Reformed. As I read this book those many years ago, my soul was made happy and I was set free from that bedeviling *and-ness* that had held my ethnic identity at arm's length from my theological identity. The two became one, and I joined the movement to make it known to all that being black is not at odds with being Reformed and being Reformed does not in the least invalidate any claims to being black.

On Being Black and Reformed was the opening gambit in an effort to see the riches of the Reformed tradition joined unselfconsciously to the riches of African America. A decade later its insights continue to be relevant to those finding their way in Christian and ethnic identity. I'm thrilled to see P&R

demonstrate wisdom and foresight in publishing this revised edition. If you want to be free from that stubborn two-ness to live in whole-person integrity as a Christian, read this book with hope and joy! It just might set you free!

Thabiti Anyabwile
Pastor, Anacostia River Church

Preface to the Second Edition

THANK you for reading (or rereading) this book. Incredibly, you are not the first. Every day I am amazed by those who say they have read it and who tell me how it has impacted their understanding of the faith. Such comments are beyond anything I anticipated when I first sat down to put pencil to paper thirteen years ago. Still, God has been pleased to use this book in the lives of many and to help them tell the story of their faith. I recall one in particular.

I remember well the day I met Timothy Byrd. It was April 2009 in Chicago at The Gospel Coalition's first national conference. Tim was walking across the hotel lobby, and I noticed him because he was a young black man in a place where young black men were scarce. Naturally, I stopped him, asked him his name, and introduced myself. When he heard my name he immediately associated it with the book *On Being Black and Reformed*. The connection was made.

We sat and talked for a while. Tim told me his story, his journey from being born into a military family in Germany to currently being on staff with Campus Outreach in South

Africa. He shared with me how he had read my book and was now passing it around to the college students and other staff members in Campus Outreach Johannesburg. At that moment I realized that God was using this book in ways and in places I would never have imagined.

Tim graciously thanked me for writing the book and relayed to me how it had greatly influenced his thinking and encouraged him in the labors God had given to him. That day we became friends and colaborers in the gospel.

On Being Black and Reformed had done it again—amazed and humbled me at the lives it has impacted for the kingdom of Christ.

When I first set out to write this book in 2001, being black and Reformed, as far as I knew, was an anomaly. The only prominent names I was aware of were Ken Jones and Carl Ellis Jr. Both of these brothers had long been holding up the standard of Reformed theology in relative obscurity. I like to say that they were Reformed before being Reformed was cool. Following their example and wanting to encourage others to openly embrace the truth of biblical and historical theology, I endeavored to write a book that would show that being black, being American, and being Reformed are not antithetical. On the contrary, the black experience in the United States is a God-ordained experience and thus fits rightly and gloriously with a Reformed theological worldview.

If you had told me that *On Being Black and Reformed* would not only still be in print thirteen years after it was first published, and still being read, but that the publisher would desire to publish a second edition, I would have asked what planet you had just arrived from—not this book, not this subject. And yet, here we are. Thirteen years later, and I am still amazed at the reach and influence the book continues to have.

Since its publication, many others have taken up the pen and written better and more expansively on this subject. Praise God! I never intended for *On Being Black and Reformed* to be the final word. On the contrary, I always hoped to spark a conversation that those smarter, wiser, and faster than me would take and run with. Thankfully, many have.

Since the book's original publication, my list of black and Reformed friends and heroes has grown exponentially. There are too many to name in this space, but a few deserve special notes. Ken Jones and Carl Ellis continue to be stalwarts, as was the late Robert Cameron. We all owe a great debt of gratitude to these pioneers in many ways.

Today, I have the privilege of laboring closely with three dear friends, Thabiti Anyabwile, Louis Love, and Philip Duncanson. My faith is stronger because of them. They are my pastors and colaborers in Christ. They are my examples. When I think of being black and Reformed, I think of their labors. They faithfully preach and practice the faith they profess. I am particularly thankful for Thabiti's contribution of the Foreword in this present volume. His words and thoughts alone make this edition worth publishing.

I would be remiss if I didn't mention the faithful brothers and sisters at P&R Publishing. For these past thirteen years, not only have they kept the book in publication, but they have also not failed to promote it and make it readily available to a new and growing generation of young, enthusiastic, creative, and influential black and Reformed-minded thinkers. I thank them for their continued confidence in this book. *May the favor of the Lord our God be upon them and establish the work of their hands; yes, establish the work of their hands!* (Ps. 90:17).

This current edition has a few additions and changes. You will notice the title has been slightly adjusted, an aforementioned foreword by Thabiti added, as well as discussion questions following each chapter, and a new appendix featuring Questions and Answers with the author. Other than these new additions, the contents have remained the same.

Lastly, I want to thank you again for reading (or rereading) this book. I pray God would be pleased to use it in your life. And, if you ever get the chance, I pray you would do me the honor and privilege of hearing how God used this book in your life. Until then, enjoy, and God bless.

Preface to the
First Edition

O F making many books there is no end" (Eccl. 12:12). So is the testimony of the Preacher, who through the wisdom of God and the seeming futility of life would have been personally acquainted with such things. There is no end to the writing of books because there is no end to the asking and the answering of questions. Humans are inquisitive creatures, living in a world full of questions that demand answers. And nowhere are the questions as pronounced as they are in history.

The study of history is a pursuit in the asking and answering of the good questions. The who, what, when, where, why, and how of history can be the source of understanding, enlightening, and resolution. For the study of history, as much as any other discipline, demands that we know who did what; when and where their actions took place; what resulted from their actions; why the outcome mattered to them; and how it can be relevant to us. This thirst for knowledge is particularly acute when we seek to understand history as the revelatory instrument of God and his character.

God is the primary mover of the universe. The study of history is fundamentally a study of God and what he is accomplishing through his moving. This is evidenced in the truth that the vast majority of the Bible is a historical record of God's dealings with his people. And the Bible is best understood when we ask the right questions and seek God to supply the right answers. Similarly, when we look at the history outside of Scripture, we must also seek to ask the right questions and thereby attain the right answers. It is to this end that I write the words contained in these pages.

On Being Black and Reformed is my attempt to ask, and posit answers to, the basic questions of the African-American experience: Where was God in the Atlantic slave trade and the subsequent slavery that was perpetrated on the African brought to what we now know as the United States? How does Christianity triumph among a people oppressed in a so-called Christian society by so-called Christians? I am aware that these questions are like multifaceted diamonds and can be approached from a variety of angles. I am hopeful, however, that the reader will find within these pages some answers, as well as some challenges, to the questions that have plagued me and many like me.

This book does not purport to have all the answers that the reader may seek. No human-authored work can. And no reader should approach any book believing that it will satisfy all his questions. With that in mind, I hope that the reader will find in these pages a pointer in the direction of the One who can answer every question and resolve every issue, the One in whom all wisdom consists—namely, the Lord and Savior, Jesus Christ. In the end, only the study that points men and women to the Savior is worthy of our admiration. I pray that by the time you've reached the end of the following material, the glories of God in Christ will have been made more plain and lovely to you.

Again, the propositions set forth in this work are in no way exhaustive. They merely attempt to stimulate others to think about and even further extrapolate their ideas. Contained in these pages is my small—yet, I pray, helpful—contribution to the conversation encouraging continued reformation and reconciliation in the church. Much more needs to be said, by minds more keen than mine. Yet its saying must be within the framework of and consistent with historic, biblical Christianity.

If there is any redeemable value in the thoughts contained in these pages, it is due in large measure to those men who saw redeemable qualities in me and endeavored to invest their time and energies. They are my teachers. They have been men of whom I was not worthy, yet God sovereignly placed them in my life at the most opportune times. Consequently, my sincerest gratitude is extended to these teachers: Barry Blackburn, who taught me to think critically; R. C. Sproul, who taught me to think clearly; Richard Pratt, who taught me to think contextually and compassionately; and Ezra Ware, who taught me that Christians must think. The words of these men have been like goads to me. They have spurred me on to pursue the deep desire of my heart—God. Their wisdom has been instrumental in my desire to honor God by pointing others to the beauty of his glory.

Also, it has been my pleasure to meet and grow extremely fond of men whose care and devotion have made them true friends. Heartfelt thanks go to three such colaborers in the quest for reformation—Sherard Burns, David Brown, and Michael Leach—faithful brothers in due season, whose ministry to me as friends and sympathizers has been incalculable; to Carl Ellis for his long and faithful work in this pursuit and his words of encouragement and critique; to Justin Taylor, for his helpful critique and his willingness as a brother in Christ to agree to disagree on some issues; to Keith Mathison and Ethan Harris, who unknowingly through conversation and example spurred me to attempt what I thought was not achievable; and to Ken

Jones, whose untiring commitment to the truths of historic Christianity has made us all more eager to take up the mantle.

I extend my sincere thanks as well to Allan Fisher and the other wonderful people at P&R Publishing for their consideration of this project and their faithful labor in seeing it through to completion.

My thanks are never complete until I voice them to Adriane, my partner and wife. We went to seminary with two small children, and four years later we left seminary with five small children. If I achieved anything in those four years, it was due to her unwavering and tireless commitment to our family and me. Daily she strives to fulfill her godward call of mother and wife. She is my example, lover, and friend.

I am aware that all the aforementioned people are in my life by the sovereign, providential hand of almighty God. Therefore, ultimately my thanks go to him, who sovereignly made me the nationality that I am, gave me the loving mother I have, revealed the theology that I hold, and imparted to me the grace in which I stand, *simul justus et peccator. Amen.*

ONE

Do We Need a
Black Theology?

Soon I will be done with the troubles of the world,
Troubles of the world, the troubles of the world.
Soon I will be done with the troubles of the world.
Goin' home to live with God.
—Negro spiritual

SEMINARY was great! Sitting under the teaching of some of the most learned minds anywhere was a humbling yet enriching experience. Being directly exposed to the theological giants of past generations and discovering how God graciously used their lives and work was an encouragement well worth the price. Even more for me, however, seminary was an awakening. It was a time when I was forced to wrestle with my consciousness of who I am as a Christian in light of my cultural context. I had to ask myself whether the experiences that contributed to making me who I am had hindered or helped me in understanding the will of God for my life. Fortunately, God used several professors, some knowingly and others unknowingly, to facilitate my spiritual quest. In fact, one incident in particular served as the catalyst for this book.

In our first required systematic theology course we discussed the doctrines of God, man, and Scripture. During the term we were required to write a research paper on a related topic of our choice. I decided to write my paper on an examination of the God of black theology.[1] My intent was to give a brief history of black theology—its roots, ideology, major proponents, etc. Then I sought to give its views of God, man, Jesus Christ, and sin. I thought it would be a provocative and unique topic (surely no one else had approached the professor with this subject in mind) and would give me an opportunity for close study of the ideas of men such as James Cone and James Washington. On receiving the paper back from my professor, I noticed that, besides the grade, he had written a question that sparked in me a deeper interest in the subject. He asked, "Is it necessary to have a black theology?"

In my paper I did not seek to validate the black theology of James Cone, James Washington, and others; nor did I try to undermine the basic premise behind the movement. In fact, I complimented the black theologians for forcing the church to grapple with issues that conservative theologians have either dismissed or denied. Perhaps the professor took my stopping short of a total denunciation of the movement as tacit approval, which was far from the truth. Whatever the case, I found his question to be thought provoking. It did not take me long to

1. The National Committee of Black Churchmen defined "black theology" thus: "Black Theology is a theology of black liberation. It seeks to plumb the black condition in the light of God's revelation in Jesus Christ, so that the black community can see that the gospel is commensurate with the achievement of black humanity" (Statement by the National Committee of Black Churchmen, June 13, 1969, quoted in James Cone and Gayraud Wilmore, eds., *Black Theology: A Documentary History*, 2 vols. [Maryknoll, NY: Orbis Books, 1998], 1:38).

come to an answer. Do we need a black theology? Do we need to speak theologically within the African-American context? Do we need to understand the African-American experience through a theological perspective that glorifies God and comforts his people? Emphatically and unfortunately, yes.

YES, EMPHATICALLY

I say "emphatically" on two accounts:

Considering the Alternative

We need a sound, biblical black theological perspective because an unsound, unbiblical black theological perspective is the alternative. A large constituency of Christianity—namely, those of African-American descent—believes the truth claims of God, Christ, and the Scriptures, but feels that the larger body of Christian theology has ignored their cultural context and circumstances. A theological perspective that fails to speak contextually to African-American life, whether orthodox or liberal, will not gain a hearing among people who have become skeptical of the establishment. The liberation theology that spawned the black theology of the sixties gained recognition and a measure of popularity not because it was biblically accurate, but because it sought to contextualize the gospel message to people who were being oppressed, marginalized, and disenfranchised.

During the socially turbulent fifties and sixties, America was forced to grapple with her own identity and how she was going to respond to the outcries of her disenfranchised. The voice that played the lead of those who yearned to be free and equal was the black voice. Black America, after years of degradation and inhumane treatment, was rising and demanding to be heard. The black voice cried for justice, equality, and self-determination. It demanded an equal voice in the political and economic system. It demanded that this inclusion be brought about by any means necessary. The means of choice came to be known broadly as Black Power.

The phrase *Black Power* expressed the social and political struggle of black America. It was *Black* because blackness was no longer viewed as a liability but rather as an asset. Out of this change arose the expression "I'm Black and I'm Proud!" It was *Power* because blacks were historically castigated and their voice in society rendered impotent. Now, authority and power were not just requested, but demanded—and where not granted, taken. But because Black Power was a socioeconomic movement, it did not give power to the whole person. Something was lacking in the soul of black empowerment. Black theology developed in an attempt to fill that gap.

Black theology sought to give a spiritual and theological framework to the pressing and distressing blight of black Americans during that turbulent period. Whereas Black Power was the political expression of self-determinism among black Americans, black theology became the theological expression of Black Power. Ironically, black theology's intent may have been noble, but its articulation and subsequent outcome has been less than noble. In fact, it has been theologically and biblically unacceptable. Yet without a solidly biblical voice setting African-American experience in a consistently redemptive and historical context, the black theology of the sixties and the subsequent ideologies based on it are the only alternatives.

Considering Cultural Contexts

We also need a sound black theology because theology in a cultural context not only has been permissible but has become normative. The tendency, however, is for the majority culture to see only its own thinking as normative—that is, to view its perspective as neutral, without any cultural trappings. Honesty demands that we recognize the ease with which theology is distinguished by culture. Noted evangelical author David Wells acknowledges this tendency.

> That American Theology has characteristics that are distinctly American should not be surprising. We readily see that the Germans and the British, the South Americans and Asians have ways of thinking about Christian faith that seem obviously German, British, South American, and Asian. In America, however, theology is apparently not affected by its context. It is not American in content or tone. It is simply theology! At least, that is what is commonly assumed.[2]

Whether it is German Lutheran, Dutch or Scottish Reformed, South American Liberation, British or American Puritanism, or even Northern and Southern Presbyterianism, theology has consistently had a distinct ethnicity or culture. To deny African Americans the right to formulate and sustain a biblical theology that speaks to the cultural and religious experience of African Americans is to deny them the privilege that other ethnic groups have enjoyed.

YES, UNFORTUNATELY

Nonetheless, I say that we "unfortunately" need a black theology. An African-American perspective on theology comes more as a reaction than as a theological initiative. It has been

2. David Wells, *No Place for Truth* (Grand Rapids: Eerdmans, 1993), 137.

made necessary by conservative Christians' failure to grapple with issues of African-American history and consciousness. This is particularly evident in the areas of racism and discrimination. The sad yet irrefutable fact is that the theology of Western Christianity, dominated by white males, has had scant if any direct answers to the evils of racism and the detrimental effect of institutionalized discrimination. The major contributors to conservative theological thought over the centuries have, consciously or not, spoken predominantly to and for white people. In fact, the unfortunate reality is that the ideologies of racism and elitism that have marred the landscape of Western civilization have had a uniquely conservative Christian flavor. Those who advocated a caste system of slavery and racial superiority in places such as the United States, England, South Africa, and India have often done so with the consent of a church defined by conservative theologians. And even though many white theologians have refuted these erroneous positions, very few have sought to positively set forth God and his providential hand in the life and struggle of African Americans.

Since the initiation of Africans to the shores of America, the destinies of white and black Americans have been inextricably intertwined. The question now is this: To what extent was this relationship destined to be that of the oppressor against the oppressed? The answer to this question, and similarly others, may not lie only in traditional American (white) theology. Rather, these questions are more satisfactorily answered in and from the context in which they are asked—thus providing a mandate for an African-American perspective on theology.

But this mandate is not without qualification. Even though there is a need for a distinctly African-American perspective on theology, the parameters of that theology must be observed: Scripture, history and tradition, and Christian experience.

Scripture, History and Tradition, and Experience

Scripture

The primary source of any sound theology is the special revelation of God contained in the Bible. Therefore, the Bible must be our ultimate authority. Whether black or otherwise, our theology is correct only insofar as it is derived from sound exegesis of the Word of God. At the foundation of this exegesis is our submission to the text of Scripture.

As faithful theologians we must approach our text humbling ourselves to its divine inspiration and submitting to its inerrancy and infallibility.[3] Because we recognize the frailty of human reason and understanding, it is incumbent upon us to assume a posture of humility and submission as we seek to pronounce ideologies about God and his creation.

Unfortunately, when we seek to prove the trustworthiness and reliability of the Bible, we often become unwitting skeptics. That is, we insist that the Bible come under the same scrutiny as any other piece of literature from antiquity. Consequently, the Bible is taken as true and reliable only after it has been shown to be the most objectively verifiable and attested-to literature we have from antiquity. While the Bible surely is verifiable and well attested, these findings do not independently prove the Bible's divine inspiration. If they did operate independently, they would essentially deny the Bible's authority. Human authorities would in effect delegate authority to the Bible after having examined it and found it worthy.

---

3. An accurate understanding of what I mean by inerrancy and infallibility can be found in the Chicago Statement on Biblical Inerrancy drafted in 1978 by the International Congress on Biblical Inerrancy.

We must not come to the Bible as skeptics, demanding that it satisfy our independent judgment. Rather, we must submit to the Bible as *our* examiner, which reveals our inadequacies of understanding. If we do otherwise, we make the Bible submit to our authority and reason, as if it receives its authority and validation from us. This must not be. Even as the people of God, we *receive* the Word. We do not authenticate the Word and thereby grant it authority. It comes to us from the source of all authority—God himself. Wilhelmus à Brakel, the much-respected seventeenth-century divine, summed it up well:

> If the Word derived its authority from the church, then we would have to hold the church in higher esteem than God Himself, for whoever gives credence and emphasis to someone's words is superior to the person who speaks them. God has no superior and therefore no one is in a position to give authority to His words.[4]

In other words, "The authority of the Word is derived from the Word itself."[5]

Furthermore, the faithful theologian is a biblical theologian. That is, he seeks to speak only where the Bible speaks and is satisfied to sit silent where the Bible is silent. As the Scriptures remind us, "The secret things belong to the Lord our God, but those things which are revealed belong to us" (Deut. 29:29). That there are issues on which the Bible does not appear to speak does not invalidate the Scriptures. On the contrary, this silence is a faithful and humbling reminder that God is God and we are not, that his ways are above our ways and his thoughts above our thoughts (Isa. 55:8).

4. Wilhelmus à Brakel, *The Christian's Reasonable Service* (Grand Rapids: Reformation Heritage Books, 1992), 30.
5. Ibid., 29.

History and Tradition

Theology must be presented with the help of history and tradition. The role of a people's heritage and tradition must never be underestimated. In many ways we are products of the theological stances and circumstances that have historically defined our communities. And though it may sometimes be necessary to broaden our perspectives and question the status quo of theological thinking, we must do so in such a way as to carefully consider that the foundations of our communities are at stake. We are not called to reinvent the theological wheel.

Whether Reformed or Arminian, Baptist or Pentecostal, Covenantal or Dispensational, theology is always best presented within a framework of heritage and tradition. A biblical African-American perspective on theology is no different. African Americans have a rich and expressive tradition from which to draw. The deeply moving spirituals forged in the cotton and tobacco fields of the antebellum South, the protestations of Richard Allen and Absalom Jones, the devotionally mystic writings of Howard Thurman, the theological expediency of Martin Luther King Jr.— our heritage is both diverse and compelling. Preachers, teachers, and books from the past that serve to enrich our study have now enriched African-American Christianity, like most other Christian communities. Yet the beauty of a biblical African-American approach to theology is that the wellspring of heritage from which to draw is not limited to African-American Christian tradition.

As much as any other segment of Christianity, the predominantly black church in America has an acute sense of its heritage. The songs we sing and the special days we celebrate are a continual reminder of the stony road trod during seemingly endless years of suffering and pain. Our songs spoke to our understanding of our worth as children of God in spite of the oppressor's attempts at dehumanization:

31

I been rebuked and I been scorned,
I been rebuked and I been scorned,
Chillun, I been rebuked and I been scorned,
I'se had a hard time, sho's you born.

Talk about me much as you please,
Talk about me much as you please,
Chillun, talk about me much as you please,
Gonna talk about you when I get on my knees.

Although recognition of our history is vitally important, this recognition often does not extend far enough. We must realize that as African-American Christians our history, as much as anyone else's, is church history. We must see that our church fathers are not just Richard Allen, Absalom Jones, and Andrew Bryan. Our fathers are also Augustine, Tertullian, and Ignatius. The songs we sing, "Were You There?" and "Swing Low, Sweet Chariot," rightly belong to us, but so do the Apostles' Creed and the Nicene Creed. We must see that our history does not begin on the Ivory Coast of Africa, but that we, like all other Christians, are the sons and daughters of Abraham, Isaac, and Jacob. Our history is church history and as such should be reflected in our theology and our preaching. As faithful theologians we must draw upon that history to ensure that we maintain a faithful course, though we chart new territory.

Making this connection with the historic Christian faith is the beauty of seeing the African-American experience within a Reformed theological framework. The Reformed understanding sees a continuity of God's work among his people. It demonstrates redemptive history not as a collection of disjointed dispensations, but rather as a continuum of covenants whereby the history of redemption is one, belonging to all the redeemed—red and yellow, black and white.

Experience

We must recognize the significant role that Christian experience plays in our understanding of theology. All human beings are, to one degree or another, a product of their experiences. These experiences over time develop into lenses through which we view the surrounding world. The opinions, ideas, biases, and prejudices that we employ at various times are in actuality the working out of our life's most impressive experiences. This is true when we formulate theology as well.

We must be honest and admit that we come to theological study with biases and prejudices. These biases, however, are not inherently a negative. In fact, the danger is not that we look at the Scriptures with a jaundiced eye, but that we think we can look at them without one. If we recognize our biases and the impact of our experiences, we can become more capable and insightful teachers. The Holy Spirit can use our experiences in our interpretation of Scripture and formulation of theology that is relevant and effective.

Experience has always been a key determiner in formulating our understanding of theology. For example, the impact of Martin Luther on Western civilization cannot be overstated. When he, in the most unassuming yet magnanimous gesture of the last millennium, nailed his 95 theses on the church door in Wittenberg, he was beckoning the church to return to the light of truth from which it had drifted so far. Yet Luther was not simply asserting theological propositions and biblical exposition; in fact, his experience as a monk frustrated with his inability to come to grips with the holy character of God in light of his own moral inadequacies caused him to delve into the biblical and theological dogma of the church. Having peered so deeply into these things, he came away with an understanding that would change the course of human history.

Our experiences, like Luther's, can be instruments for the discovery of divine truth. God is not averse to using our experiences in order to reveal his will for us and drive us to confirm these experiences through his Word, the Bible. Unfortunately, with any conduit of knowledge, too much dependence on one element leads to a distortion of the truth. An overemphasis on God's communicating with our rational faculties leads to a rationalistic Christianity that is void of emotional content. Likewise, an overemphasis on God's communicating through our experiences leads to an experiential Christianity that is void of rational boundaries. The unfortunate errors of nascent black theology were rooted in the assumption that experience should be the primary source of truth. The result of this experience-driven approach is that church history and even the Scriptures are relevant only insofar as they coincide with and corroborate my experience as an African American. In other words, that which does not validate my experience and indeed empower me against the oppressive white establishment is of no use in communicating the revelation of God to me.

We see that experience overemphasized is fraught with error, potential and realized. Nevertheless, though experience has been erroneously overemphasized in traditional black theology, in attempting to formulate a more scriptural approach to the African-American perspective on theology we must be careful not to underemphasize the role of experience.

No theologian can directly influence the black church more effectively than a black theologian. His experiences as a black man in America provide him with a credible and sympathetic voice. Yet his awareness of his cultural existence must be tempered with the more immediate reality of his existence in the kingdom of God, which is not bound by cultural and social categories. His identity as a Christian must inform his identity as an African American, not vice versa. A black theology that is both biblical and culturally credible will take the experiences of black people seriously and address a theology in which experience is viewed not above but concomitant with Scripture and community. I am convinced that such theology is best articulated and maintained within the Reformed theological tradition. Thus, I suggest that "reforming" the black theological experience is not only possible but also, more importantly, necessary.

My goal in *Black and Reformed* is to redeem and reform our perspective on the black American experience through the most legitimate lens available, theology—in particular, biblically based and historically grounded Reformed theology. The term *Reformed* is meant to identify with the theological formulations of the Reformed theological tradition. The Reformed understanding of God, man, sin, salvation, and the Scriptures is the most coherent and veritable of all views. It provides the most comprehensive, biblically consistent paradigm for interpreting a providentially orchestrated history.[6]

In reflecting on my theological experiences, I respectfully give deference to those men who bravely paved the way for black

6. For a brief introduction to Reformed theology and history, I suggest reading Ronald H. Nash, *The Meaning of History* (Nashville: Broadman & Holman, 1999); J. I. Packer, *Knowing God* (Downers Grove, IL: InterVarsity Press, 1973); David G. Hagopian, ed., *Back to Basics* (Phillipsburg, NJ: P&R Publishing, 1996); David N. Steele and Curtis C. Thomas, *The Five Points of Calvinism* (Phillipsburg, NJ: Presbyterian and Reformed, 1963); Michael S. Horton, *Putting Amazing Back in Grace* (Grand Rapids: Baker, 1991); R. C. Sproul, *Grace Unknown* (Grand Rapids: Baker, 1997); James R. White, *Potter's Freedom* (Amityville, NY: Calvary Press Reformed Publishing, 2000).

theology. Yet the forerunners of this theology, though noble in their intentions, failed to maintain a faithful and high view of Scripture. These failures led to a nebulous view of man, sin, history, Christ, God, and the Scriptures. Men like James Cone, James Washington, Deotis Roberts, Gayraud Wilmore, while sincerely seeking to articulate their faith in an African-American context, failed to maintain the integrity of scriptural doctrines that are pivotal and indispensable to the historic Christian faith.[7] And though we are indebted to these men for awakening the Christian theological community to its neglect of black America, we must not let that cloud our primary goals as theologians—to glorify God and to comfort the saints.

The black theology birthed in the sixties did provide a temporary balm for souls at a time when black people needed it most. It not only shook the conscience of mainstream theology and forced it to see that it had taken a myopic view, but also awakened the conscience of black people and gave them the assurance that they were created in the image of God and that he had a design for their existence. But by denying the essentials of the historic Christian faith and divine inspiration of Scripture, that salve became toxic, infected with nationalism and a self-destructive humanism. In fact, it became little more than a mirror of much of the racist white theology against which it posited itself. Black theology not only failed to give lasting comfort to souls, but also by default failed to glorify God. Ultimately, a theology that fails to reach one of these goals inherently fails to reach either of them.

A black Reformed theological perspective on history has the primary goal of glorifying God. We are confident that as it

7. You can see their positions on these doctrines in James Cones's sentient work *A Black Theology of Liberation* (Maryknoll, NY: Orbis Books, 1990) and the two-volume documented analysis of the development of black liberation theology, edited by James Cone and Gayraud Wilmore, *Black Theology: A Documentary History*.

does so, it will in turn be a comfort to the people of God. The Reformed black theologian's prayer is an echo of the psalmist's:

> Let the words of my mouth
> and the meditation of my heart
> Be acceptable in Your sight,
> O LORD, my strength and my Redeemer. (Ps. 19:14)

Discussion Questions

1. What is the relationship between theology and cultural context?
2. Why is it important to formulate an African-American perspective on theology?
3. What is the significance of Scripture, history, tradition, and experience in formulating any theology?

TWO

A Case for Reformed Theology

God of our weary years,
God of our silent tears,
Thou who has by thy might,
Led us into the light.
—James Weldon Johnson

THE account is given of a slave gravedigger and his young helper in antebellum Mississippi and their encounter with a white stranger. The gravedigger asks the stranger:

"Massa, may I ask you something?"
"Ask what you please."
"Can you 'splain how it happened in the fust place, that the white folks got the start of the black folks, so as to make dem slaves and do all de work?"
The younger helper, fearing the white man's wrath, broke

in: "Uncle Pete, it's no use talking. It's fo'ordained. The Bible tells you that. The Lord fo'ordained the Nigger to work, and the white man to boss."

"Dat's so. Dat's so. But if dat's so, then God's no fair man!"[1]

Whether this account is apocryphal or not, we don't know. But what is true is the anecdotal nature of the account and that advocates of Reformed theology have been characterized as dyed-in-the-wool predestinarians, who see God as the divine despot who wields a subjective, irrational sovereign hand over all creation. This caricature of Reformed theology, unfortunately, dominates the popular thinking and has caused many to speak of Reformed theology in derisive and sometimes mocking terms. One typical nineteenth-century illustration of the seemingly ubiquitous attacks on the Reformed understanding of salvation is the following doggerel by Elias Smith, "On Predestination":

If all things succeed
Because they're decreed
And immutable impulses rule us;
Then praying and preaching,
And all such like teaching,
Is nought but a plan to befool us.

If destiny and fate,
Guide us this way and that
As the coachman with bits guides his horses;
There's no man can stray,

1. Nathan O. Hatch, *The Democratization of American Christianity* (New Haven, CT: Yale University Press, 1989), 171.

But all go the right way,
As the stars in their different courses.

If this be the way,
As some preachers say,
That all things were order'd by fate;
I'll not spend my pence,
To pay for nonsense,
If nothing will alter my state.[2]

Though such poems are humorous, their creativity is surpassed by the misunderstanding and blatant ignorance concerning the truths of Reformed theology they seek to bemoan.

The truth is that Reformed theology is intensely biblical theology. In fact, it was Charles Spurgeon, the famous nineteenth-century Baptist preacher in England, who unashamedly stated that Reformed theology is merely a nickname for biblical Christianity. It is a biblical theology in that it maintains a high view of Scripture and the need for a consistently God-centered approach to interpreting Scripture. The admirable desire to interpret Scripture consistently and clearly has led those in the Reformed strain to formulate the essential qualities of Reformed thinking in a way that is readily grasped. Therefore, what is popularly known as Reformed theology can be summarized in the five points of Calvinism.

2. Ibid., 139. Those who attack Reformed theology have recently found their voice in books such as *The Other Side of Calvinism* by Laurence Vance. According to the misguided assertions of Mr. Vance, "Nothing will deaden a church or put a young man out of the ministry any more than an adherence to Calvinism. . . . There is no greater violator of every hermeneutical, contextual, analytical, and exegetical interpretation of Scripture than Calvinism" (rev. ed. [Pensacola, FL: Vance, 1999], viii). Another example is the less-than-accurate musings of Dave Hunt in *What Love Is This: Calvinism's Misrepresentation of God* (Sisters, OR: Loyal Publishing, 2002).

The Five Points of Calvinism

The five points are represented in the acrostic TULIP, as follows:[3]

Total Depravity

When Adam fell into sin, he plunged all his progeny into sin (Rom. 5:12). The Bible teaches by both practice and precept that all humankind is under the command of sin (Gen. 6:5; Jer. 17:9; Rom. 3:9–12). The pervasiveness of this sin is total (2 Chron. 6:36; Job 15:14–16). The totality of which we speak is not to the effect that humans are as bad as they could possibly be, but rather that sin has corrupted every area of human existence: mind, body, and soul. To this end humans are totally depraved, "sold under sin."

Unconditional Election

According to the Scriptures, God predetermined before the foundations of the world those sinners whom he would save through the atoning work of Christ on the cross (Eph. 1:4; Rev. 13:8). This election was unconditional in that it was based solely in his good pleasure and in accordance with his sovereign will (John 15:16; Rom. 9:11–13, 16; 10:20). The unconditionality of election is necessary when one understands the depth of human depravity.

Limited Atonement[4]

In accordance with the perfect will of God, the sacrificial

---

3. For a more exhaustive study of the history of Calvinism and the five points of Calvinism, see Curt Daniel, *History and Theology of Calvinism* (Dallas: Scholarly Press, 1993); David Wells, ed., *Reformed Theology in America* (Grand Rapids: Baker, 1997); J. I. Packer, "Introductory Essay," in John Owen, *The Death of Death in the Death of Christ* (London: Banner of Truth, 1959).

4. Though *Limited Atonement* is used to make the acrostic more aesthetically

work of Christ had a definite design (Rom. 5:10; 2 Cor. 5:18–19, 21; 1 Peter 3:18). The atonement was designed so that those who were elected by God unto salvation would be saved. The work of Christ is not to be thought of as only making salvation possible, but as actually accomplishing the salvation of all those appointed unto salvation (1 Thess. 5:9–10). Therefore, we discern that the atonement was particularly designed for the redemption of God's people (Matt. 1:21; John 6:35–40; 10:11–18).

Irresistible Grace

This aspect of God's salvific work speaks to the efficacious nature of God's salvation. All those whom God has appointed unto salvation (Acts 13:48) not only receive the outward call of the gospel (all who hear the preached Word thus receive this external calling), but also will inevitably receive the inward call of the Holy Spirit (Acts 16:14; Rom. 8:30; 2 Tim. 1:9). By this work of the Holy Spirit they are drawn to God for salvation (Matt. 11:25–27; John 6:37, 44–45; 10:4, 14–16). This regenerating work of God in the heart of a sinner is not thwarted or compromised. For if God determines to save someone, who can deter his purpose? Thus we can say that his supernaturally imparted grace cannot be resisted.

Preservation of the Saints

The final point is a fitting culmination of the previous points. It states that God preserves those who come to faith through the efficacious work of God in redemption until their final redemption is accomplished (Eph. 4:30; Col. 3:3–4; 2 Tim. 1:12). Those whom God has called and justified by his grace will be glorified to

---

appealing, the notion of limits on the work of God stirs mixed emotions in people. A better phrase for describing this aspect of God's salvific work is probably *Particular Redemption*.

his glory (Rom. 8:29–30, 35–40), and none of those whom he has ordained unto salvation will be lost (John 6:35–40; 10:27–30).[5]

Though the five points are an accurate summation of the biblical doctrine of salvation, sadly they are usually all that most people know about the teachings of Reformed theology. As stated above, Reformed dogmatics is biblical dogmatics. The Scriptures are what inform Reformed beliefs. And though I heartily affirm the five points of Calvinism and find over-whelming biblical as well as logical evidence for their veracity, in formulating my own simple approach I suggest that the case for Reformed theology may be made in terms of three biblical truths: the sovereignty of God, the sinfulness of humans, and the sufficiency of Christ.

THE SOVEREIGNTY OF GOD

Perhaps no single attribute of God has come under more attack and scrutiny than his sovereignty. It is explicitly attacked by theologians who insist that there are limits to the exercise of God's sovereignty in the world as we know it.[6] It is also under implicit attack daily by Christians who fail to acknowledge God not only as Creator, but equally as the One who sustains and ordains all that comes to pass. They speak of God as knowing all things, but in the same breath suggest that he is not in control of all things. They politely suggest that God surrenders some aspects of his sovereignty that humans might exercise free will. The modern popular view of God is no more than a distorted caricature of the

5. This point commonly goes by the title "perseverance of the saints," which is accomplished by God's preserving power and grace.
6. The most popular recent books along these lines are *The Openness of God*, ed. Clark Pinnock, and *The God Who Risks: A Theology of Providence* by John Sanders.

biblical deity. The modern God proclaimed in many pulpits is a sickly invalid who is apparently unable to accomplish anything without the initiative and prerogative of humans.

Recently I heard a preacher proclaim that Satan's work is being accomplished every day, while God's work remains undone because we refuse to get after it. Such statements inherently attribute more power and authority to Satan than the Bible allows and simultaneously rob God of the sovereign, omnipotent control over his creation upon which the Bible insists. A more accurate assessment of God's sovereignty is found in the Westminster Confession of Faith, echoed by the Baptist Confession of 1689: "God from all eternity, did, by the most wise and holy counsel of His own will, freely, and unchangeably ordain whatsoever comes to pass."[7] This assertion is consistent with the biblical understanding concerning God's sovereign rule over all things:

> For His dominion is an everlasting dominion,
> And His kingdom is from generation to generation.
> All the inhabitants of the earth are reputed as nothing;
> He does according to His will in the army of heaven
> And among the inhabitants of the earth.
> No one can restrain His hand
> Or say to Him,
>   "What have You done?" (Dan. 4:34–35)

Accordingly, when we speak of God's sovereignty, we are speaking of his kingly rule over all his creation. There is no place to which this sovereignty does not extend and no activity or affair in his creation over which he is not governor.

---

7. Westminster Confession of Faith, 3.1 (see also Baptist Confession of 1689, 3.1).

He Is Sovereign over Humans

> A man's heart plans his way,
> But the LORD directs his steps. (Prov. 16:9)

> The king's heart is in the hand of the LORD,
> Like the rivers of water;
> He turns it wherever He wishes. (Prov. 21:1)

> There are many plans in a man's heart,
> Nevertheless the LORD's counsel—that will stand. (Prov. 19:21)

> The LORD stirred up the spirit of Cyrus king of Persia, so that
> he made a proclamation throughout all his kingdom. (Ezra 1:1)

> The LORD kills and makes alive;
> He brings down to the grave and brings up.
> The LORD makes poor and makes rich;
> He brings low and lifts up. (1 Sam. 2:6–7)

In speaking to Belshazzar, Daniel states that

> the God who holds your breath in His hand and owns all your
> ways, you have not glorified. (Dan. 5:23)

He Is Sovereign over Nations

> If there is calamity in a city,
> will not the LORD have done it? (Amos 3:6)

> And I indeed will harden the hearts of the Egyptians, and they
> shall follow them. (Ex. 14:17)

For it was of the LORD to harden their hearts, that they should come against Israel in battle, that He might utterly destroy them, and that they might receive no mercy, but that He might destroy them, as the LORD had commanded Moses. (Josh. 11:20)

Woe to Assyria, the rod of My anger
And the staff in whose hand is My indignation.
I will send him against an ungodly nation,
And against the people of My wrath
. . . .
Shall the ax boast itself against him who chops with it?
Or shall the saw magnify itself against him who saws with it?
As if a rod could wield itself against those who lift it up,
Or as if a staff could lift up, as if it were not wood. (Isa.
        10:5–6, 15)

He Is Sovereign over the Elements

I Myself am bringing the flood of waters on the earth, to destroy from under heaven all flesh in which is the breath of life. (Gen. 6:17)

He sends out His command to the earth;
His word runs very swiftly.
He gives snow like wool;
He scatters the frost like ashes;
He casts out His hail like morsels;
Who can stand before His cold?
He sends out His word and melts them;
He causes His wind to blow, and the waters flow. (Ps.
        147:15–18)

I also withheld rain from you,
When there were still three months to the harvest.
I made it rain on one city,
I withheld rain from another city. (Amos 4:7)

When Jesus spoke to the storm-driven seas with the words, "Peace, be still!" his disciples responded, "Who can this be, that even the wind and the sea obey Him!" (Mark 4:39, 41).

He Is Sovereign over Physical Afflictions

So the LORD said to him, "Who has made man's mouth? Or who makes the mute, the deaf, the seeing, or the blind? Have not I, the LORD?" (Ex. 4:11)

The LORD will strike you with the boils of Egypt, with tumors, with the scab, and with the itch, from which you cannot be healed. The LORD will strike you with madness and blindness and confusion of heart. (Deut. 28:27–28)

It is clear that the Scriptures teach by precept and practice that God is sovereign in the universe. And nowhere is Scripture more insistent upon God's sovereignty than in the realm of salvation. Yet this is the most neglected aspect of his sovereign rule, even among those who claim to enthusiastically affirm the other areas of his sovereignty. An examination of Scripture should leave no doubt about God's final rule even in the matter of salvation.

He Is Sovereign over Election

The electing prerogative of God in the matter of salvation, as in the above-mentioned aspects, is proved over and over again by precept and example.

For you are a holy people to the LORD your God; the LORD your God has chosen you to be a people for Himself, a special treasure above all the peoples on the face of the earth. The LORD did not set His love on you nor choose you because you were more in number than any other people, for you were the least of all peoples; but because the LORD loves you. (Deut. 7:6–8)

Before I formed you in the womb I knew you;
Before you were born I sanctified you. (Jer.1:5)

Salvation is of the LORD. (Jonah 2:9)

The wind blows where it wishes, and you hear the sound of it, but cannot tell where it comes from and where it goes. So is everyone who is born of the Spirit. (John 3:8)

You did not choose Me, but I chose you and appointed you that you should go and bear fruit, and that your fruit should remain. (John 15:16)

And as many as had been appointed to eternal life believed. (Acts 13:48)

For He says to Moses, "I will have mercy on whomever I will have mercy, and I will have compassion on whomever I will have compassion." So then it is not of him who wills, nor of him who runs, but of God who shows mercy. (Rom. 9:15–16)

. . . just as He chose us in Him before the foundation of the world, that we should be holy and without blame before Him in love, having predestined us to adoption as sons by Jesus

Christ to Himself, according to the good pleasure of His will. (Eph. 1:4–5)

The Scriptures are clear. God does not simply know all things, as most Christians would suggest, but more accurately has decreed all things. In other words, God is not an impotent deity who must wait for his creatures to act in order for his purposes to be accomplished. Rather, his creatures act according to his divine decree, and nothing occurs in all of creation that is not in accord with his ultimate will. This is especially true of salvation. That salvation is necessary is because God decreed it before the worlds began (Eph. 1:4). That salvation is possible is because God has determined it to be so (Acts 2:23). That salvation is attained is because God has appointed certain ones unto it (Acts 13:48). And that salvation is completed is because God has predetermined that it would be (Rom. 8:29–30). Again the confessions are insightful in this account:

> God who, in infinite power and wisdom, has created all things, upholds, directs, controls and governs them, both animate and inanimate, great and small, by a providence supremely wise and holy, and in accordance with His infallible foreknowledge and the free and immutable decisions of His will. He fulfills the purposes for which He created them, so that His wisdom, power and justice, together with His infinite goodness and mercy, might be praised and glorified.[8]

Perhaps no attribute of God is more relevant to our understanding of the purpose for our lives than his sovereignty. That he is sovereignly working his plan in our lives for his glory and our good is our only comfort in life and in death.

8. Baptist Confession of 1689, 5.1 (see also Westminster Confession of Faith, 5.1).

THE SINFULNESS OF HUMANS

When I was in college, a non-Reformed professor made the point, "Total depravity, that is, the sinfulness of humanity, is the one Calvinistic doctrine that is objectively verifiable." Indeed, we need only turn on the local news channel or glance at the front page of the local newspaper to see the depths to which humans are willing to go to display the universality of our ignoble sinful disposition. Whether it is kids killing kids, drug-addicted mothers giving birth to addicted babies, murderous police officers, corrupt politicians, or serial killers (and the list goes on *ad infinitum*), we are daily brought to the awareness of the degenerate nature of the human heart.

Furthermore, the preferred means of entertaining ourselves also reveal our sinful desires. Popular music, movies, sitcoms, and soap operas are too frequently a flagrant display of our lack of conformity to the law of God. We daily entertain ourselves with the reckless defiance of the Ten Commandments as most of the popular music and movies seek to advance their popularity by discovering new ways of taking the Lord's name in vain, committing adultery, lying, stealing, murdering, and coveting. Yet we, unlike many politicians and so-called social watchdogs, need not blame the entertainment industry for creating a degenerate society. The media simply feeds us what we most desire to consume: sin. Before the advent of television, movie screens, radio, or newspapers (believe it or not), the Bible plainly told us that the human condition is totally in the throes of sinful behavior.

From Socrates to Sartre, humans have tried to diagnose their own propensity for self-destruction. Every age has borne new ideas about the driving force behind human desires and the seemingly indomitable presence of evil. Yet long before popular philosophical or sociological discourse on the subject, the Scriptures explained this ever-present tendency in humans toward evil deeds. Their diagnosis is sin.

There is no questioning that the Scriptures represent humans as being in rebellion against and even at war with God. The Bible is a history of humankind's rebelling against the law of God and living a life of sin. After the initial disobedience of our first parents in the Garden of Eden, it is not long before we are shown the evil that lies within the heart of all. In chapter 4 of Genesis, Cain rises up and slays his own brother, Abel, in cold blood. From there on, sin is manifested in the Bible as a progressively menacing player in the grand drama of redemption:

> Early biblical sin rises in ominous crescendo—Adam and Eve's juvenile pride and disbelief triggering disobedience, scapegoating, and flight from God (Gen. 3:4–5, 10, 12–13). Their first child then extends his parents' trajectory: Cain blames and kills his brother Abel, launching the history of envy and fratricide within the human family.[9]

The Scriptures make it plain that our lawlessness is based in our innately sinful disposition. In other words, we are born that way. The ignoble idea that humans are born in sin may not be popular in Christianity today, but it is inherently biblical. According to Scripture, all who are born into this world inherit the sinful nature and resultant guilt of Adam. As Paul asserts in Romans 5:12, "Therefore, . . . through one man sin entered the world, and death through sin, and thus death spread to all men, because all sinned." Furthermore, we see the innate aspect of sin reflected in the words of David. As David ponders his

9. Cornelius Plantinga Jr., *Not the Way It's Supposed to Be: A Breviary of Sin* (Grand Rapids: Eerdmans, 1999), 30.

fall from grace and his willingness to compound transgression upon transgression, he realizes that his aptness to compound sin is more than just the result of learning—it lies far deeper, even in the recesses of the soul: "Behold, I was brought forth in iniquity, and in sin my mother conceived me" (Ps. 51:5). David furthers the indictment in Psalm 58:3: "The wicked are estranged from the womb; they go astray as soon as they are born, speaking lies."

Anyone who has ever been around children can testify to a child's tendency toward sin. We need not teach our children to be selfish; rather, we must teach them the advantages of sharing. Children naturally manifest the ways of the world and the flesh. It is necessary to instruct them in the ways of the Lord. The scriptural admonition is clear: parents are to teach their children to do right, to "bring them up in the training and admonition of the Lord" (Eph. 6:4), which is not their natural bent. Yet the Bible not only condemns humans as sinners by birth, but even more emphatically illustrates that we are sinners by practice.

One of the fascinating aspects of the history of sports is that the greatest athletes are usually the ones who work the hardest. While nature and genetics play a major role in dividing the great athletes from the good ones, a careful examination would prove that the best were usually those who practiced the most.

Most experts would agree that Michael Jordan was the greatest basketball player the world has ever seen. His career is a virtual highlight film over which even his professional colleagues were left grasping for adjectives. Yet we know that many of the physical attributes that made Jordan successful were genetically passed along. He was born with the genetic makeup to grow six feet, six inches tall and to have hands large enough to manipulate a basketball. In other words, he was born that way. Being born with these traits and others, however, is not the sole reason for his greatness. Michael Jordan was great because he practiced hard at his craft.

The intensity with which Jordan approached practice was legendary. It is said that though he was the most gifted athlete on his team, he was nevertheless the first to arrive for practice and the last to leave. Many of his teammates report having to request that he tone down the intensity for fear of injury. Jordan realized that the perfection of his skills depended not only on the exercising of God-given ability, but also on the practice and repetition needed to develop those skills beyond the ordinary. We may conclude that not only was he great because he was born with certain traits, but he was great because he diligently practiced to develop those traits.

Similarly, the Bible asserts that the greatness of our sin is due first to our innate predisposition and second to our willingness to practice sinning relentlessly. Job's friend Eliphaz expounded on our ignoble condition when he said,

> What is man, that he could be pure? And he who is born of a woman, that he could be righteous? If God puts no trust in His saints, and the heavens are not pure in His sight, how much less man, who is abominable and filthy, who drinks iniquity like water! (Job 15:14–16)

The Preacher stated, similarly, that no one escapes the throes of sin: "For there is not a just man on earth who does good and does not sin" (Eccl. 7:20). And the apostle Paul summed up our despicable condition when he stated,

> For we have previously charged both Jews and Greeks that they are all under sin.
>   As it is written:

"There is none righteous, no, not one;
There is none who understands;
There is none who seeks after God.
They have all turned aside.
They have together become unprofitable.
There is none who does good, no, not one." (Rom. 3:9–12)

Indeed, the scriptural assessment of humanity's sinful condition is demonstrated to us daily. It seems that our appetites for the immoral grow even as we believe we are becoming more sophisticated and advanced as a civilization. The ironic thing is that humans have tried to curtail this self-destructive behavior by applying various philosophical theories:

- sociological (put humans in the right environment and they will become better people),
- economic (give humans the right economic resources and advantages and they will prove morally capable),
- educational (supply the proper intellectual stimulation and academics and humans will lift themselves up from the mire of immorality).

All these theories sound noble and have some advantages, but as the Bible asserts and history testifies, none have satisfactorily cured the human plight of sin. There is not a sociological structure in which we have not seen the most heinous examples of humans' inhumanity to humans. Give sinners more money and economic opportunities and they will only show themselves more resourceful and creative in exercising their sinful predisposition. Simply educate the immoral and they will inevitably demonstrate that immorality has no boundaries. As someone once said, "If you take a fool who is stealing railroad ties and educate him, he will only come back and steal the entire track." No sociological, economic, or educational program will cure our ignoble condition. Not only does the Bible give us the most accurate diagnosis of humankind's sinfulness; it also gives us the only cure—the life, death, and resurrection of Jesus Christ. The only one sufficient unto the work of conquering seemingly unconquerable sin is Jesus Christ.

THE SUFFICIENCY OF CHRIST

It has become commonplace and indeed faddish for athletes today to begin their post victory remarks with the refrain, "I want to thank God. . . ." While I don't have an aversion to thanking God for achievement of one's life's goals, I am patiently waiting for someone to emerge from the loser's locker room and say, "I want to thank the Lord in my loss." I am confident that the modern tenor of Christianity has little use for a God who is glorified in our failures and shortcomings. Yet the Bible clearly teaches that the sufficiency of Christ extends to all of life. Those who praise God only in the good, joyful successes of life are asserting that Christ is sufficient only when goals are reached. But those who would lay a solid foundation for understanding biblical truth must embrace the fact that Christ is sufficient unto all things (2 Cor. 12:1–10).

He is sufficient for our *justification* (1 Cor. 6:11; Rom. 5:9). He has won our pardon. He has borne our guilt. The punishment for our sin was put upon him, and our hope of eternity was secured. And while the world is guilty and hopeless, the beloved in Christ are guiltless and hopeful.

He is sufficient for our *sanctification* (1 Cor. 1:2, 30; Heb. 10:10; 13:12). He has supplied our holiness. He has been made unto us perfection and righteousness. When God sees the beloved, he sees Christ.

He is sufficient for our *glorification* (Rom. 8:29–30; 1 Cor. 15:20, 23, 49). Christ is being formed in us. He has supplied the image to which we are attaining. God will glorify the beloved because Christ is glorified.

This is the work of Christ in our salvation. It is salvation past, present, and future. And Christ is sufficient unto it all. He justified us in the past. He sanctifies us in the present. He will glorify us in the future. The works of Christ in justification, sanctification, and glorification are biblical essentials to our life in Christ. They are the core truths that ground our relationship with God—a relationship defined by incomparable forgiveness. Our greatest need in our relationship with God is forgiveness. And our greatest need in our relationship with each other is forgiveness. The basis for both is found in the all-sufficient work of Christ.

Forgiveness is the hallmark of Christianity. It is indeed that which separates Christianity from all other forms of religious practice. It is the summation of Christ's work on our behalf. I once asked a Muslim friend, "What do you do with sin? If your God is such a righteous, just, and impeccable God, how can he accept humans who are altogether unrighteous, unjust, and sinful? How are your sins forgiven?" He responded that God in his all-powerful and sovereign character categorically forgives sin at his whim, simply upon the request of the Islamic adherent. While this view of God and sin is desired and even promoted by most religious people, it is an inherently contradictory view. A God who would arbitrarily forgive sin, cancel moral debt, and leave the unjust unpunished could not himself be a righteous judge. Would we call a human judge who allowed the guilty to go free a righteous judge? While this may be the characteristic of the God of Islam, it is nowhere reflective of the God of the Bible.

Abraham, in reflecting on the righteous character of God, asked the rhetorical question, "Shall not the Judge of all the earth do right?" (Gen. 18:25). The God of the Bible is a just, righteous, and holy God. We are reminded that he does not overlook sin: "God is not mocked; for whatever a man sows, that he will also reap" (Gal. 6:7). He will not leave the guilty and unjust unpunished: "The Lord is slow to anger . . . and will not at all acquit the wicked" (Nah. 1:3). Therefore, if we are going to be in fellowship with him, our sins must be atoned for and our moral debt paid. This is in fact the work of Christ in our redemption. He, in his life of perfect righteousness, fulfills for those who believe the life they could never live (Rom. 5:19). Furthermore, in his sacrificial atonement on the cross, he paid the moral debt of our sins by dying the death that sin demanded of us (Rom. 6:23). In codifying the biblical truth of Christ's substitution, the Baptist Confession of 1689 states:

> By His perfect obedience to God's law, and by a once-for-all offering up of Himself to God as a sacrifice through the eternal Spirit, the Lord Jesus has fully satisfied all the claims of divine justice. He has brought about reconciliation, and purchased an everlasting inheritance in the kingdom of heaven, for all those given to Him by His Father (John 17:2; Rom. 3:25–26; Heb. 9:14–15).[10]

And having received the atoning work of Christ on our behalf by faith (Rom. 5:1), we now stand before God having had our sins erased and clothed in perfect obedience. Hymn writer Charitie Lees Bancroft summed up this beautiful truth with the words:

> Because the sinless Savior died,
> My sinful soul is counted free.

10. Baptist Confession of 1689, 8.5.

For God the Just is satisfied,
To look on Him and pardon me.[11]

Biblical Christianity alone sets forth the desperate state of sinful humanity and the all-sufficient work of Christ as the cure. The work of Christ not only grounds our forgiveness by God, but also grants the means for our forgiving others (Matt. 6:12; Eph. 4:32).

In Christ we are forgiven and we find the means of forgiving others. No greater power is known to humankind than the power of forgiveness. When a person has been wronged and has been the victim of intentional harm, there is no greater means of disarming the wrongdoer than to forgive. Forgiveness is not natural. It runs counter to our natural inclinations of self-preservation and self-fulfillment. Yet we are never more like Christ, and thus more Christian, than when we are operating in Christlike forgiveness. And nowhere is this work of forgiveness more decisively needed than in race relations in America. In fact, the civil rights movement has arguably been the most dramatic display in recent years of the reconciliatory power of forgiveness wrought by the life and death of Christ.

It should not be lost to us that the civil rights movement was undergirded by Christian principles. Not only did the church supply the primary leadership (Martin Luther King Jr., Ralph Abernathy, John Lewis, Andrew Young, and others were all ordained ministers), it also supplied the primary places of meeting and fellowship. The church buildings were the obvious choices amid the ever-present threat of terrorism. Yet even more than leadership and location, the church supplied the most important element of all, the principle of love—the means of forgiving one's enemies.

11. "Before the throne of God above."

The power of the civil rights movement was in the power of Christianity. The power of Christianity is in the ability to display uncommon forgiveness. Our Lord reminded us,

> But I say to you, love your enemies, bless those who curse you, do good to those who hate you, and pray for those who spitefully use you and persecute you. (Matt. 5:44)

This was the ethic that fueled the civil rights movement and the rhetoric of the leadership. Martin Luther King Jr. summed it up with these eloquent words,

> To our most bitter opponents we say: "We shall match your capacity to inflict suffering by our capacity to endure suffering. We shall meet your physical force with soul force. Do to us what you will, and we shall continue to love you. . . . Throw us in jail, and we shall still love you. Send your hooded perpetrators of violence into our community at the midnight hour and beat us and leave us half dead, and we shall still love you. But be ye assured that we will wear you down by our capacity to suffer. One day we shall win freedom, but not only for ourselves. We shall so appeal to your heart and conscience that we shall win you in the process, and our victory will be a double victory."[12]

The willingness to love and forgive with such zeal is possible only in light of the work of Christ. He alone provides the grounds for such action by forgiving so freely and magnanimously.

Reformed theology is biblical theology because it asserts uncompromising biblical truth. There is no comprehending

12. Martin Luther King Jr., *Strength to Love* (New York: Harper and Row, 1963), 48.

of biblical truth without its being undergirded by the under-standing that before a holy, righteous, and sovereign God, sinful and depraved humans have no means of being accepted and counted among the blessed unless they are found in Christ, who alone supplies all that is necessary for a relationship with the one true God. God is sovereign. Humans are sinful. Christ is suffi-cient. This is the message communicated by Reformed theology because it is the message contained in the Bible.

So what does Reformed theology have to offer the African-American Christian? It offers a biblically consistent hermeneutic[13] and a paradigm for understanding the providential hand of God in the African-American experience. It fact, it is the only perspective that seeks to understand God in the full extent of his sovereignty while maintaining the biblical mandate of human responsibility. Most theological and philosophical perspectives err on one position or the other. True Reformed theology seeks to hold both, as the Bible does, without diminishing God's sovereignty or absolving humans of responsibility. As tenuous as these positions may be, no other theology has the inner consistency and necessary dexterity of Reformed theology.

African Americans should identify with Reformed theology because it is the theology of Joseph when he declared to his broth-ers, "You meant evil against me; but God meant it for good . . ." (Gen. 50:20). It is also the theology of Job when, in struggling to resolve God's providence in his suffering, he declared, "Though He slay me, yet will I trust Him" (Job 13:15). Ultimately it is the theology of Paul, who summed up the above statements in Romans 8:28: "And we know that all things work together for good to those who love God, to those who are the called accord-ing to His purpose." All things can work out for good because

13. A method of interpreting Scripture.

God has decreed all things. And since God is the ultimate Good, all things work out for God, which is glory for him and in turn good for us.

My prayer is that all my brothers and sisters—black, white, brown, red, and yellow—would come to see the beauty and glory in the doctrines of grace and see that they form the parameters for understanding the deepest theological question facing us, namely, how a holy and righteous God could condescend to fellowship with and even redeem unholy and depraved sinners.

> Heavenly Father, great is your faithfulness toward us. You have endeared yourself to us for all time. While we were unlovable, you chose to love us. While we were untouchable, you chose to touch us. While we were unreachable, you chose to extend your hand and reach us. Lord, it is to this display of incomprehensible love and mercy that we humbly bow our knees. In the presence of such overwhelming grace, what could be the response of unworthy beings but the silencing of their tongues and the covering of their heads? Father, our deepest yearning is that you would cover us, that you would lift up our heads and purify our tongues. Then, Lord, in uncovering us, you would welcome us into your presence. In lifting up our heads, you would allow us to know you even as we are known. In purifying our tongues, you would give us the fulfillment of our hearts' most pressing desire—true, uninterrupted, unadulterated praise.

Discussion Questions

1. In what ways have you heard Reformed Theology characterized?
2. What are the Five Points of Calvinism?
3. In what ways does the Bible assert the sovereignty of God?
4. How does the Bible characterize the sinfulness of men and women?
5. In what ways is the sufficiency of Christ important for the Christian?

THREE

The Church from Chains

When Israel was in Egypt's land,
Let my people go.
Oppressed so hard they could not stand,
Let my people go.
—Negro spiritual

T HE African-American church is a case study in the Reformed, biblical understanding of truth. We see in the development of the African-American church a testimony to the sovereignty of God. He orchestrates and conducts the affairs of human history so as to accomplish his determined plan in bringing a people to himself. We see the sinfulness of humanity. The existence of the African-American church is also an indictment upon those who engaged in the Atlantic slave trade and those who refused to openly welcome their newly converted African brothers and sisters into their fellowships. Also, we see demonstrated the sufficiency of Christ. He alone is able to work graciously within the context of such sinful and inhumane treatment to bring about a redeemed people for his praise and glory. The African-American church is a poignant reminder that our understanding of doctrinal truth must never be divorced from our understanding of history and how our God reveals himself. It demonstrates that African-American Christians' very existence is without a doubt the supernatural work of God's providence.

The African-American church is an enigma. It is an institution whose existence is unlikely and unpredictable. How could African-American men and women embrace the same Christ that their oppressors professed? Despite the worst intentions of many and because of the best intentions of others, the African-American church, as an institution, is arguably the most indomitable in American history. God literally raises his church up from chains.

THE ONSLAUGHT OF SLAVERY

As early as the thirteenth century, Europeans had begun to discover the wealth of resources to be pillaged from inland Africa. For the next two centuries, there would be no expense spared in obtaining the gold and ivory indigenous to the African continent. Yet as valuable as gold and ivory were, the Europeans became convinced of the exceeding value of human cargo and began the trafficking of African men and women. This became especially true as the European powers pushed westward across the Atlantic into North and South America of today.

In 1440, the Portuguese were the first to discover the profitability of importing Africans as servants. They brought to their shores from Africa, along with their other cargo, 20 Africans for the purpose of selling them as slaves.[1] Subsequently, as the Portuguese began colonizing what is today Brazil and other regions

1. Mark Galli, "A Profitable Little Business," *Christian History 53* (16, no. 1): 20.

of South America, they concluded that the workforce needed for the successful development of their Brazilian colonies would be best supplied by importing Africans as slave laborers.[2] Following the inauspicious lead of Portugal, Spain, France, and England began a mass raping of Africa of her most valuable resource as each raced for colonial superiority in the New World. According to one seventeenth-century chronicler, "The Portuguese served for setting dogs to spring the game, which as soon as they had done was seized by others."[3] Yet despite the efforts of the others, it was not long before Britain became the chief European trafficker in slaves. According to one source:

> By the early 1700s, English traders dumped about 25,000 Africans on the other side of the Atlantic every year. By about 1770, it had risen to 50,000, half of what all Europe exported. By 1787 the numbers were down, but Britain was still the European leader in transports, with 38,000 slaves annually (France was second with 31,000).[4]

As noted above, justification for the actions of the state was commonly sought from the church. Therefore, it is not surprising that many consciences were soothed when justification for the Atlantic slave trade was proposed on missionary grounds. According to some, the forced enslavement of Africans, though prima facie inhumane, was actually the most humane thing that

2. Ibid.

3. Willem Bosman, quoted in Hugh Thomas, *The Slave Trade* (New York: Simon & Schuster, 1997), 48. That is, the Portuguese were like hunting dogs pointing to the prey.

4. Ibid., 21. William Pitt the Younger, addressing the House of Commons in April 1792, rebuked the English for their continued indulgence with the evil of the slave trade. He declared, "No nation in Europe . . . has . . . plunged so deeply into this guilt as Great Britain" (quoted in Thomas, *The Slave Trade*, 235).

the Christian Europeans could do because it introduced the heathen natives to the truth of the gospel. Gomes Eannes de Azurara, a Portuguese observer of the mass importation of Africans onto the shores of Portugal, believed that the Africans were the ones who received the greater privileges in the venture, "for though their bodies were now brought into some subjection, that was a small matter in comparison of their souls, which would now possess true freedom for evermore."[5] Over the next few centuries many in the church would echo Azurara's sentiments as the debate over slavery intensified.

As England began colonizing the New World, the primary labor forces for establishing productive colonies were African slaves. The initial influx of slaves to America under the banner of Britain was slow. The concern of most colonists was minor agriculture, and most of the Africans were either indentured servants or domestic servants. Not until the discovery of the cash crops of rice, tobacco, sugar, and cotton in the southernmost colonies did the importation of Africans as slaves really soar and regular slave trade in America begin.

The Carolinas were the first to discover this need. With the rise of the tobacco market in the Carolinas, it was widely believed that "these new tobacco plantations could not be served by a few indentured servants; and that white men did not work well in the rice fields."[6] Therefore, the market for African slaves grew tremendously.

> In his *Natural History of North Carolina*, published in 1737, John Brickell declared that slaves were reckoned "the greatest riches in these parts," and that the planters "were at great pains

5. Albert Raboteau, *Slave Religion: The Invisible Institution in the Antebellum South* (New York: Oxford University Press, 1978), 96.
6. Thomas, *Slave Trade*, 258.

to lay in store gold and silver with which to purchase Negroes in the West Indies and other places."[7]

With the growing number of Africans in the colonies, the need to observe the Christian duty of evangelizing them became more pressing.

King Charles II, feeling that his English colonies were falling behind Spain, Portugal, and France in missionary zeal toward their slaves, ordered his Council for Foreign Plantations to consider how

> slaves may best be invited to the Christian faith, and be made capable of being baptized thereunto, it being to the honor of our Crown and of the Protestant religion that all persons in any of our dominions should be taught the knowledge of God, and be made acquainted with the misteries [sic] of salvation.[8]

While the monarchy in England was declaring that bringing the kingdom of God to the captives was the ultimate good in the slave trade, the conduct of the colonial planters revealed a different motive. Introducing the good news of the gospel to those whom they had made their servants was definitely a consideration of the colonial planters. It was a consideration, however, only insofar as it did not interfere with the primary objective of slavery—economic profiteering.

EVANGELICAL NEGLIGENCE

Though evangelical pronouncements spewed from the mouths and pulpits of colonial America, the true and abiding

7. Ibid.
8. Raboteau, *Slave Religion*, 97.

determinant for slavery was not missionary, but monetary. The intent of the planters and slave traders was not evangelistic, but the increase of their earthly treasure. Anything, even the propagation of the gospel, that interfered with this primary objective was either rationalized away or denounced. This mind-set is demonstrated in the several excuses often set forth for the neglecting of slave conversion.

First, among the colonial planters, some feared that conversion, and subsequent baptism, might emancipate their slaves. The laws of Britain and the canons of the church were vague at best in speaking to this potential situation. The rights of baptized citizens of the Crown and the church had not been overtly communicated. Therefore, some exercised doubt and apprehension at the potential status of baptized slaves. Along these lines, "would-be missionaries to the slaves complained that slaveholders refused them permission to catechize their slaves because baptism made it necessary to free them."[9] Evidently, the colonists did not want to take any chances of losing their investment even if they gained a brother or sister in Christ. Therefore, "by 1706 at least six colonial legislatures had passed acts denying that baptism altered the condition of a slave 'as to his bondage or freedome' [sic]."[10] Though these acts seemed to clear the air concerning the state of baptized slaves' liberty, other excuses soon developed.

A second reason entertained to explain the lack of zeal toward slave conversion was the consumption of time. Most colonists believed that a candidate for baptism must first be instructed in the principles of the faith. Catechizing a candidate, however, took time, which entailed an economic loss. With the sunup-to-sundown work regimen that typified plantation life, there

9. Ibid., 98.
10. Ibid., 99.

was little, if any, time for religious instruction. Sunday was the one day available for such instruction (if the plantation owner allowed for it).[11] But "even when the slaves were not forced to work on the Sabbath, finding time for religious instruction was problematic, since the minister had 'work enough from the white folks on his hands.'"[12]

A third reason for the neglect of the slaves' spirituality was the widely propagated belief that Africans were too bestial and brutish and therefore incapable of religious instruction. This misconception was due in large measure to the language barrier that existed between the transplanted Africans and the English colonists. So firmly was the conviction held in some places that the Virginia House of Burgesses wrote to the Governor in 1699 that concerning the conversion of Africans it was necessary to distinguish between those born in the colonies and those imported:

> The Negroes born in this country are generally baptized and brought up in the Christian religion; but for Negroes imported hither, the gross bestiality and rudeness of their manners, the variety and strangeness of their languages, and the weakness and shallowness of their minds, render it in a manner impossible to make any progress in their conversion.[13]

The inherent racist ideology displayed in this type of thinking made it virtually impossible for the necessary love and concern for the unconverted slave to develop. Bishop George Berkeley, commenting on this racist apathy, believed that this "irrational contempt for the blacks, as creatures of another species, who

11. Some masters insisted that their slaves work even on the Sabbath. Among those who didn't, Sunday was the one day that slaves had available to tend to their own needs.
12. Raboteau, *Slave Religion*, 99.
13. Ibid., 100.

have no right to be instructed or admitted to the sacraments; has proven to be a main obstacle to the conversion of these poor people."[14] The insistence that Africans lacked the intellectual capabilities or the spiritual faculties necessary for spiritual affections (after all, if they were beasts, they could not have souls) again greatly hindered the spread of the gospel to these needy people. But even though it was greatly hindered, it was not altogether thwarted. Many in the colonies did endeavor to bring the gospel to the slaves.

EVANGELICAL DILIGENCE

In the face of social and political opposition, some preachers insisted that the propagation of the gospel, and the conversion of the slaves in particular, was more important than maintaining the status quo of the slavocracy. To this end, Cotton Mather, a Puritan divine, wrote a tract entitled *The Negro Christianized* (1706). In it he argued for the inclusion of Negroes among those favored by God to receive the good news of the gospel. He exhorted the slaveholders among his readers:

> Show yourselves men and let rational arguments have their force upon you, to make you treat, not as brutes but as men, those rational creatures whom God has made your servants. . . . Yea, if thou dost grant that God hath made of one blood, all nations of men; he is thy brother, too.[15]

It is important to note that in Mather's analysis of the slaveholder's neglect in particular and the church's in general, he raises

14. Ibid.
15. Ibid., 101.

the issue of the rational capabilities of Negroes.[16] Mather and others attempted to dispel the racist myth of African rational incapability that kept the gospel from being proclaimed to the Negro. Among them was Edmund Gibson, bishop of London. In 1727 he wrote a letter to the colonial planters in which he admonished them to "encourage and promote the instruction of their Negroes in the Christian faith" because they "have the same frame and faculties with yourselves."[17]

Despite the missionary zeal of some, few African Americans, whether slave or free, were Christians prior to the Revolutionary War. Not until the revival movements in the last quarter of the eighteenth century did the growth of Christianity among the African Americans really take off. Specifically, it was the unfettered zeal of the Baptists and the Methodists that produced the greatest and longest-lasting results. During the years immediately following the War of Independence, the church

16. Immanuel Kant and David Hume had argued that the Negro lacked rational faculties, thus making equality with whites unthinkable. Kant and Hume's influence on the thinking of the colonists is unmistakable. Henry Louis Gates Jr., in *The Norton Anthology of African-American Literature* (New York: W.W. Norton & Company, 1997), quotes Kant as saying, "The negroes in Africa have by nature no feeling that rises above the trifling. Mr. Hume challenges anyone to cite a single example in which a Negro has shown talents, and asserts that among the hundreds of thousands of blacks who are transported elsewhere from the countries, although many of them have been set free, still not a single one was ever found who presented anything great in art or science or any praise-worthy quality, even though among the whites some continually rise aloft from the lowest rabble, and through superior gifts earn respect in the world. So fundamental is the difference between these two races of man, and it appears to be as great in regard to mental capacities as in color. The religion of fetishes so wide-spread among them is perhaps a sort of idolatry that sinks as deeply into the trifling as appears to be possible to human nature. A bird feather, a cow horn, a conch shell, or any other common object, as soon as it becomes consecrated by a few words, is an object of veneration and of invocation in swearing oaths. The blacks are very vain but in the Negro's way, and so talkative that they must be driven apart from each other with thrashings" (p. xxx).

17. Raboteau, *Slave Religion*, 101.

in America experienced great growth, much of it among the slave population. There are thought to be several reasons for phenomenal African-American growth among the Baptists and the Methodists.

First, the Baptists and Methodists of the eighteenth century welcomed slaves into their communions and condemned the practice of slavery (though their attitudes would change dramatically in the nineteenth century as the slavery debate intensified).[18] Unlike men such as Samuel Davies and George Whitefield, who sought the conversion of slaves but did not speak for their freedom,[19] Methodists such as Freeborn Garrettson and Francis Asbury not only displayed zeal for slave conversion, but spoke forthrightly of their equality and right to freedom. According to one historian, "After freeing his own slaves in 1775, Garrettson, a native of Virginia, faced regular threats because he laced his evangelistic preaching with attempts to 'inculcate the doctrine of freedom.' "[20] Furthermore, the sermons coming from the Methodists excited a yearning for freedom and a sense of equality in the slaves. According to one slave, "I had recently joined the Methodist church and from the sermon I heard, I felt God had made all men free and equal, and I ought not to be a slave."[21]

Second, the Baptist and Methodist congregations exemplified a fresh and experiential Christianity. Unlike the Presbyterians

18. Nathan O. Hatch, *The Democratization of American Christianity* (New Haven, CT: Yale University Press, 1989), 102.

19. Arnold Dallimore, biographer of George Whitefield, relates: "In those days it was frequently asked, 'Does the Negro have a soul?' and Whitefield gave the first widely-heard positive reply that the black man was basically no different from the white man. Nevertheless, we cannot but regret that he did not come to the conviction that slavery was utterly evil and demand in his powerful eloquence that 'liberty and justice' be granted to all men, black as well as white" (*George Whitefield* [Wheaton, IL: Crossway, 1990], 81).

20. Hatch, *Democratization*, 103.

21. Ibid., 102.

and the Anglicans, whose sermons were full of theoretical and theological language, the Baptists and Methodists proclaimed a Christianity that was readily understood and immediately experienced. One slave is reported to have lamented:

> My mistress and her family were Episcopalians . . . so we went to the Episcopal Church. But always came home as we went, for the preaching was above our comprehension, so that we could understand but little of what was said.[22]

Richard Allen, the founder of the African Methodist Church, explained Methodism's appeal among the African Americans thus: "The Methodists were the first people that brought glad tidings to the colored people . . . for all the other denominations preached so high flown that we were not able to comprehend their doctrine."[23]

A third, and perhaps most significant, reason for the Baptist and Methodist attraction was the willingness of these less formal movements to develop and promote African-American preachers. The emergence of the African-American preacher is not to be considered lightly. Before the Revolution, the African-American preacher was virtually nonexistent. Yet following the war, the Baptists and Methodists recognized the invaluable role that the African-American preacher could play in the conversion of slaves. The inability of some to read or write was not a hindrance for the Baptists and Methodists. These denominations "prized spiritual

22. Ibid., 104.
23. Ibid. "While the Anglican clergyman tended to be didactic and moralistic, the Methodist or Baptist exhorter visualized and personalized the drama of sin and salvation, of damnation and election. The Anglican usually taught the slaves the Ten Commandments, the Apostles' Creed and the Lord's Prayer; the revivalist preacher helped them to feel the weight of sin, to imagine the threats of Hell, and to accept Christ as their only Savior" (Raboteau, *Slave Religion*, 132).

vitality more than education in clergy, so if a converted African-American showed a gift for preaching, he was encouraged to preach, even to unconverted whites."[24]

The ability of slaves to go and hear someone with whom they could readily identify must not be taken for granted. The message of the white preacher was often mixed with hypocrisy and cruelty.[25] Yet the African-American preacher brought with him a perceived integrity and trustworthiness rare among the white preachers. The Baptists and Methodists took advantage of this scenario and surpassed the Anglicans and Presbyterians in missionary success. In fact, the Anglican missionaries in Virginia lamented the success of the Baptists among the slaves and expressed concern that Baptists often let "Negroes speak in their meetings."[26] Charles Colcock Jones, a prominent Presbyterian evangelist and himself a slaveholder, noted, "In general the Negroes were followers of the Baptists in Virginia and after a while, as they permitted many colored men to preach, the great majority of them went to hear preachers of their own color."[27]

24. Mark Galli, "Defeating the Conspiracy," *Christian History*, 62 (18, no. 2): 13. In fact, so impressed were some whites with the preaching of "Uncle" Jack, an African-born slave and Baptist convert, that they purchased his freedom and settled him on a farm, where he preached for 40 years and even saw the conversion of his former master's son (Raboteau, *Slave Religion*, 135).

25. "One slave reported that his master served him communion at church in the morning and whipped him in the afternoon for returning to the plantation a few minutes late" (Galli, "Defeating the Conspiracy," 15).

26. Raboteau, *Slave Religion*, 134.

27. Hatch, *Democratization*, 106. Jones illustrates the contradiction with which Christian slaveholders were willing to live. He wrote extensively on the subject of catechizing slaves and worked dutifully in this area. But he "did not view his mission as a threat to the institution of slavery, believing that slaves must be transformed into a 'civilization people' before they could commend themselves to their masters as worthy of freedom" (D. G. Hart and Mark Noll, eds., *Dictionary of the Presbyterian and Reformed Tradition in America* [Downers Grove, IL: InterVarsity Press, 1999], 134).

The numerical success of the Baptists and Methodists among the African Americans was unparalleled. In fact, it so stifled the efforts of the Presbyterians and Anglicans that "well into the nineteenth century Episcopalians and Presbyterians were still wringing their hands about their failure to Christianize their own slaves."[28] Nevertheless, the growth of African-American Christianity was that of an institution within an institution. That is, African-American Christians were subject to the ordinances of larger white ecclesiastical bodies. They could never be self-determined or own the property on which they worshiped—until one fateful Sunday in April 1787 at St. George Church in Philadelphia.

EVANGELICAL DIVISION

St. George Methodist Episcopal Church was a prominent Methodist church in Philadelphia and had long welcomed African Americans into its fellowship. In 1786, Richard Allen, a prominent black preacher in the Methodist movement, had come to Philadelphia to preach at St. George. Though he had intended to stay in Philadelphia only for the preaching engagement, he made Philadelphia his home. A year later, St. George had just finished a remodeling project in which a balcony had been constructed. Whereas the seating prior to the construction of the gallery had not been segregated, the gallery allowed for a shift in the seating. And unbeknownst to Allen and other African-American congregants, they would no longer be allowed to sit on the main floor.

On that Sunday following the construction, Richard Allen and Absalom Jones walked into the sanctuary to take their

28. Hatch, *Democratization*, 102.

regular seating. As the service began they knelt in prayer, only to have Jones be pulled up by one of the trustees, who told him, "You must get up—you must not kneel here."[29] Under the threat of being physically removed, Jones and Allen left the main sanctuary, and according to Allen, they "all went from the church in one body and they were no more plagued with us in that church."[30]

In 1794, Richard Allen and Absalom Jones founded two African-American churches in Philadelphia: St. Thomas's African Episcopal Church (the first black Episcopal church in America) under the leadership of Absalom Jones, and Bethel Methodist Church under the leadership of Richard Allen. The black population seized the opportunity to remove themselves from the institutional racism of the established white churches and flocked to the two newly started works. "An estimated 40 percent of Philadelphia's fifteen hundred blacks had joined one or the other by the turn of the century, a level of church participation possibly twice that of comparable white laboring classes."[31]

Following the great influx of members into his church, Richard Allen and other African-American leaders in the Methodist movement thought it best to formally organize themselves apart from what they had experienced as second-class citizenry in Methodism. In 1816 the African Methodist Episcopal Church (AME) was organized as a self-governing body, and Richard Allen was consecrated as its first bishop. Thus was born the move toward independence from the often racist and neglectful white churches in America. Today the AME Church stands as the oldest independent, predominantly black denomination in America. Bethel Church in Philadelphia stands as the oldest parcel of real

29. Will Gravely, "You Must Not Kneel Here," *Christian History*, 62 (18, no. 2): 35.
30. Ibid.
31. Hatch, *Democratization*, 109.

estate continuously owned by African Americans. In fact, Bishop Allen and his wife Sarah are interred in the church's lower level.[32]

Someone has said that the most segregated time in America is at 11 o'clock on Sunday morning. The evidence for this unfortunate reality is all around us. The issues that racially divide Christians in America today are complex and multifaceted, existing on several levels (political, economic, social, as well as religious). But without question the segregation we witness each Sunday had its root cause in the refusal of white Christians to welcome their brothers and sisters of a darker hue at a time when these brothers and sisters had no alternative. Undoubtedly, it was through the missionary zeal of colonial America that African Americans were introduced to the gospel and through God's grace brought into the kingdom of God. Yet once in the kingdom, these same African Americans found segregated seating and second-class citizenry. Inevitably, it became necessary to leave such abuse so that worship could be experienced unimpeded. Ironically, the segregation we witness today is in fact the segregation that segregation itself produced.

The blacks' response to such hypocrisy-laden Christianity could have been a complete rejection of the one true God in Christ. Yet instead of rejecting Christ, African Americans rejected this brand of Christianity, separating what the Bible taught about Christian virtue from what so-called Christians practiced. None other than Frederick Douglass eloquently set forth the necessity of slaves' distinguishing the Christianity of Christ from that of slaveholding and slavery-approving America:

> Between the Christianity of this land, and the Christianity of Christ, I recognize the widest possible difference—so wide,

32. Gravely, "You Must Not Kneel Here," 36.

that to receive the one as good, pure, and holy, is of necessity to reject the other as bad, corrupt, and wicked. . . . I am filled with unutterable loathing when I contemplate the religious pomp and show, together with the horrible inconsistencies, which everywhere surround me. We have menstealers for ministers, women-whippers for missionaries, and cradle-plunderers for church members. The man who wields the blood-clotted cowskin during the week fills the pulpit on Sunday, and claims to be a minister of the meek and lowly Jesus. The man who robs me of my earnings at the end of each week meets me as a class-leader on Sunday morning, to show me the way of life, and the path of salvation. He who sells my sister, for purposes of prostitution, stands forth as the pious advocate of purity. He who claims it a religious duty to read the Bible denies me the right of learning to read the name of God who made me. He who is the religious advocate of marriage robs whole millions of its sacred influence, and leaves them to the ravages of wholesale pollution. The warm defender of the sacredness of the family relation is the same that scatters whole families,—sundering husbands and wives, parents and children, sisters and brothers,—leaving the hut vacant, and the hearth desolate. We see the thief preaching against theft, and the adulterer against adultery. We have men sold to build churches, women sold to support the gospel, and babies sold to purchase Bibles for the *poor heathen! all for the glory of God and the good of souls!* The slave auctioneer's bell and the church-going bell chime in with each other, and the bitter cries of the heartbroken slave are drowned in the religious shouts of his pious master. . . . The dealers in the bodies and souls of men erect their stand in the presence of the pulpit, and they mutually help each other. The dealer gives his blood-stained gold to support the pulpit, and the pulpit, in return, covers his infernal business with the garb of Christianity. Here we have religion and robbery the allies of each other—devils dressed in angels' robes, and hell presenting the semblance of paradise.[33]

Douglass's analysis is both telling and compelling. If not for the providential hand of God overriding the frailty of human actions, the development of an African-American church would never have occurred and the grace of God may never have been realized among these people. Yet despite this inauspicious beginning, the African-American church did thrive. Despite the hypocrisy of her spiritual sister, the African-American church has experienced grace above measure. In this, the analogy of Joseph's story is apropos.

The deceit and hypocrisy of Joseph's brothers could have been the demise of Joseph had not God maintained a sovereign hand on his life. And even though they could be held completely culpable for his enslavement and imprisonment in Egypt, Joseph discerns a higher power working in the affairs of humans (Gen. 45:1–8). Thus, when confronting his older brothers concerning their sin, he precisely sums up the inauspicious beginning of the African-American church: "You meant evil against me, but God meant it for good . . ." (Gen. 50:20).

Walter Goodman, historian, has said, "The experience of slavery must trouble America's conscience until its effects are eradicated, its injustices somehow redeemed." These sentiments ring true for the church in America as well. Yet I am convinced that no understanding of theology and history will more capably facilitate a reconciling of the history and theology of the African-American church than will Reformed theology. Only

33. Frederick Douglass, *Narrative of the Life of Frederick Douglass*, in Frederick Douglass: Autobiographies, Literary Classics of the United States (New York: Library of America, 1994), 97.

in Reformed thinking do we get a clear picture of God sovereignly working within the realm of sinful humans to bring about the existence of a dynamic church and, more importantly, the redemption of all those who believe. In fact, if Christians of various races would examine history from the perspective of a sovereign God ordaining and orchestrating all events for his glory, we would find that we have more in common than not.

A Common Heritage

It has been said of the United States and Great Britain that we are people separated by a common language. Similarly, it could be said of the distinctive black and white churches in America that we are a people separated by a common heritage. America is the most diverse nation on the earth. The experience of each racial group is as diverse as the individuals that make up those groups. Some came here as political refugees, while others were religious exiles. Some came as entrepreneurs, while others came as servants and chattel. Some came on ships seeking freedom, and others came on ships having lost their freedom. Yet as Jesse Jackson is fond of saying, "No matter what ship you came here on, we're all in the same boat now." And as it is with our temporal, nationalistic kingdoms, so it is more so with the eternal kingdom of God.

The kingdom of God comprises a diversity of people with a common heritage. This heritage is not primarily black, white, red, yellow, or brown, but is a heritage rooted in redemptive history. And the history of redemption is not black history, white history, or African or European history. It is God's history. Therefore, any understanding of God's activity in history must begin and end with the fact that though the individuals are diverse and varied, the God who sovereignly reigns over history is one and the same—yesterday, today, and forever. The context of the experience with God may change and be variously expressed, but if the experience is genuinely with the true and living God, the outcome is predictably and gloriously the same. Two examples may clarify this for us.

In the late 1800s, Horatio Spafford was a successful white businessman in Chicago. He held many prominent pieces of real estate along the north shore of Lake Michigan. Unfortunately, the tragic and infamous fire of 1871 practically destroyed all of Spafford's holdings. Many of his friends lost everything they owned. It was devastating, to say the least.

Spafford was overwhelmed with the loss and calamity. Consequently, he sought to establish a more profound relationship with Jesus Christ. As a result, he decided that the best avenue for the fulfillment of this quest would be to leave the hustle and bustle of Chicago and move to Jerusalem. He booked his entire family, wife and four daughters (they had lost their only son years earlier to scarlet fever), on a ship from New York to France. At the last moment, however, he was called back to Chicago to tie up some loose business deals. He told the family to continue on, planning to meet them in France in a couple of weeks. Little did Spafford know that he had just seen his family alive together for the last time.

As the ship made its way across the Atlantic, it met with a terrible accident. In midocean, the ship collided with another ship and sank within minutes. When the survivors reached land, Spafford's wife sent him a telegram that contained only two words: "Saved alone." Spafford had lost all four daughters.

As he sailed to France to meet his wife, Spafford was made aware of the point in the voyage at which his daughters had been lost. As he stood on the bridge contemplating the loss of his children, he was inspired to write these words:

When peace like a river attendeth my way,
When sorrows like sea billows roll;
Whatever my lot, Thou hast taught me to say,
It is well; it is well with my soul.

"It Is Well with My Soul" is a most beloved hymn in American Christianity. It was born out of a time of pain and distress, neither of which is foreign to white, black, brown, or any other racial designation of Christianity. In fact, it is the common ground on which God works in the lives of all his children.

Move ahead 60 years. Again the scene is Chicago. A talented young black musician named Thomas Dorsey was making a name for himself by playing blues music throughout the Midwest. He had moved to Chicago from rural Georgia in the early 1920s in the hopes of taking the blues industry by storm. His talents were undeniable. He wrote more than two hundred blues songs and worked with some of the most prominent blues singers and musicians of his day.

But as the Depression set in, Dorsey realized that he was empty and longing for more fulfillment. So he turned to the only hope he knew, the faith that his parents had presented to him as a child growing up under the preaching of his father in Georgia. By 1932 Dorsey had all but left the blues scene and was playing gospel music throughout the area.

In August of that year, he and his young wife were expecting their first child any day. Reluctantly, Dorsey accepted an invitation to play at a revival meeting in St. Louis. Planning to be gone only a few days, Dorsey drove to St. Louis to play. He had been in St. Louis for only two days when he received a telegram that informed him that his wife had delivered a baby boy, but that she had not survived the delivery. Distraught, Dorsey had some friends drive him back to Chicago. When he returned, he found a weak newborn baby who would die only hours after his arrival.

Dorsey was naturally overwhelmed by this tragedy. At the age of 33 he had lost his family. For weeks the grief rested upon him until one day as he sat at the piano, he began to reflect on his circumstances and the words began to flow:

Precious Lord, take my hand,
Lead me on; let me stand.
I am tired, I am weak, I am worn.
Through the storm, through the night
Lead me on to the light.
Take my hand, precious Lord; lead me home.

"Precious Lord, Take My Hand" is one of the most beloved gospel songs in the African-American gospel tradition. There are few hymnals today where these words are not found.

Thomas Dorsey and Horatio Spafford were separated by time and culture. They were separated by race and position. Yet the providential experience of both with the one true God revealed a common heritage—one of faith and devotion.

The black experience and the white experience in America are different and often in conflict. We need not deny this. As Christians, however, we can affirm that though our experiences may be contextually different, our membership—indeed our citizenship—is in the same kingdom, the kingdom of God. It is the eternal kingdom where the citizens are called and united under the same Spirit, the same Lord, and the same faith.

O Heavenly Father, we stand in awe of your wonder, your inexpressible power, and your inconceivable mercy. For only you, O God, could have such unlimited power and yet such mercy and grace. From your hand comes both cursing and blessing. From your hand comes both life and death. And yet, Lord, who could accuse your hands of being uneven? Who could say that there is injustice with you? You have made all things necessary and have worked all for good. Is it not through cursing that we have indeed been blessed? Is it not by way of death that we have come to know life? Is it not by your mercy that we have the privilege of experiencing your grace? Holy One, we would be consumed, yes, even destroyed, were you not merciful in all your ways. You alone are faithful. You alone are true.

Discussion Questions

1. With such an ignoble beginning, what impresses you most about the black church in America?
2. In colonial America, many were opponents of evangelizing slaves. What were their reasons?
3. The Baptists and Methodists were the first to see success in evangelizing slaves. What were some of the reasons for this success?
4. At one time Reformed theology was the dominant theological perspective of African-American Christians. How can it be so once again?
5. "Black and white churches in America are a people separated by a common heritage." In what ways should this heritage brings us together more than separate us?

FOUR

On Being Black
and Reformed

'Twas mercy brought me from my Pagan land,
Taught my benighted soul to understand
That there's a God, that there's a Saviour too:
Once I redemption neither sought nor knew.
—Phillis Wheatley

THE Reformed tradition is one of the richest theological traditions produced by the church. It considers within its lineage such theologians as Augustine of Hippo, Martin Luther, John Calvin, John Knox, Jonathan Edwards, B. B. Warfield, Francis Schaeffer, James I. Packer, and others. It has produced such preachers as John Bunyan, Charles Spurgeon, and D. Martyn Lloyd-Jones. It has been the theology of missionaries and evangelists such as William Carey, David Livingston, and George Whitefield. And it has inspired hymn writers such as Isaac Watts, William Cowper, Augustus Toplady, and Sir John Newton. Through the theological reflection of these men and others, the church has been enriched and a tradition has been sustained.

In Bible college and seminary I discovered the rich and biblically vibrant theology of the Reformed tradition, and the Bible was opened to me in new and refreshing ways. Theology became invigorating, and I was able to see continuity between the church now and the saints of old. Experientially, the sovereignty of God had a greater impact not only on my understanding of redemptive history, but also on my life in particular. For the first time I became aware of his intimate involvement in the details of life, especially mine. It thus drew out of my worship a more intense and substantive praise.

Yet something was missing. As much as I desired it, an intimate connection with Reformation history was hampered by my inability to identify culturally with those who stand as its magisterial architects. I was convinced of the truth of Reformation doctrine, but experientially I was impoverished because of a lack of history with which I could identify. Then I made a second and perhaps more important discovery: the tradition of black religion and the legitimacy of a black perspective on theology. I then committed myself to bringing together the richness of the two traditions to maximize my Christian experience.

Traditionally, it has been thought that the black religious experience is incompatible with the Reformed tradition. This is partly because many who espoused Reformed teaching in eighteenth- and nineteenth-century America were reluctant to come to grips with the inherent evils of slavery. According to George Marsden, a Reformed theologian and scholar, "In the deep South, Reformed people were adamantly opposed to any interference with the practice of black slavery and emphasized aspects of the tradition that favored confining the activities of the church to strictly 'spiritual' issues."[1] Furthermore, many were perceived as advocating an acceptance of the societal status quo.

For example, the Reformed doctrine of predestination, though biblical, has become associated with Reformed theology in a negative way. It has been erroneously understood as more fatalistic than biblical. It is believed as a result that many African Americans in the eighteenth and nineteenth centuries "found little place for predestination in their understanding of Christianity."[2] The blacks' aversion to biblical predestination was especially felt by the Reformed or Calvinist preachers of the day, and the evangelistic fervor of Reformed Christians among African Americans was thus greatly reduced. The result of this lack of initiative on the part of the Reformed heritage has been the scarcity today of predominantly black churches in the Reformed tradition.

Yet the truth is that Reformed preaching is the best means for putting the African-American experience into historical as well as biblical context. In fact, my experience as an African-American Christian was not crystallized until I discovered the richness of Reformed theology and I coupled it with the indomitable character of African-American Christians.

As I grew up in the church, I assumed that my theological heritage and tradition was strong. My mother and grandmother were present every Sunday morning. For me they were theology. They were the expression of Christ, the manifestation of God-likeness. The songs we sang were not projected onto an overhead video screen. Nor were many of them to be found in the pew hymnals. Neither the organist nor the pianist could be seen poring over sheets of music, yet their fingers seemed

1. George M. Marsden, "Introduction: Reformed and American," in *Reformed Theology in America*. ed. David F. Wells (Grand Rapids: Baker, 1997), 6.

2. Nathan O. Hatch, *The Democratization of American Christianity* (New Haven, CT: Yale University Press, 1989), 171.

to intuitively dance over the keys. Despite the lack of formalism, the fervor with which we expressed these songs was not diminished, nor was the clarity of content obscured. The words of such songs as "I Know It Was the Blood"[3] and "Down by the Riverside"[4] were a part of us, and their melodies resonated within us. Through them theology came alive and faith was given expression. Through them I saw my heritage of faith, and it was rich. Yet it was not until I traveled to Bible college and later to seminary that I really understood the span of my heritage and the richness of my tradition.

As I made my way through predominantly white Christian institutions, Atlanta Christian College and Reformed Theological Seminary, it became increasingly apparent to me that my experience as a Christian in America and my experience as a black in America were not the same. It may seem obvious to many—since we in America are fond of drawing a distinction between the "church" and the "state"—that to be American does not mean to be Christian. But many Americans have long held to the fallacious notion that America is a Christian nation. They insist that she was birthed amid the flames of Christian persecution and nurtured herself with the insistence upon freedom of religion.

Yes, Christian sentiments and tokens of faith are woven throughout our society, from the inscriptions on currency, to the oaths taken in court, to the national holidays of Easter, Christmas, and Thanksgiving. Furthermore, the church in America has long seen men such as George Washington, Thomas Payne, and John Adams not only as patriots but also as men of faith and

3. *I know it was the blood / I know it was the blood / I know it was the blood for me. / One day when I was lost / He died upon the cross / And I know it was the blood for me.*
4. *I'm gonna lay down my burdens / Down by the riverside / down by the riverside / down by the riverside. / I'm gonna lay down my burdens / Down by the riverside / I'm gonna study war no more.*

Christian virtue. Yet even if the experience of America has been a Christian experience, it has been a white Christian American experience. This was brought home to me in seminary when confronted with the question of the legitimacy of a black theology. To raise that question is to assume that theology has historically had no cultural or racial perspective.[5] Yet if honesty prevails, we must admit that American theology has lacked cultural or racial diversity and has been the poorer for it.

Theology is something that the church has been actively engaged in since its inception. America has made its contributions to theological thinking and has built some prominent theological institutions over the years (Princeton, Harvard, Yale, Westminster, Fuller, etc.). Yet in formulating this theology, it inevitably did so through the experience of white America. Though these theologians undoubtedly believed that their theology was simply an outworking of the biblical record, they were writing from their experience as white American males. It has been correctly stated that "theology is contextual language—this is, defined by the human situation that gives birth to it. No one can write theology for all times, places, and persons."[6] Bruce Fields, conservative scholar and professor of systematic and biblical theology at Trinity Evangelical Divinity School, echoes that conviction when he writes:

> All theology is in some sense a "local theology," that is, a system of thought that emerges from the interplay of the gospel, the church, and culture. . . . The church has a double-lensed

5. Though I have major disagreements with James Cone, he does make a legitimate point in reference to criticism of a black theology: "It is not surprising that those who reject blackness in theology are usually whites who do not question the blue-eyed white Christ" (*A Black Theology of Liberation* [Maryknoll, NY: Orbis Books, 1990], 8).

6. Ibid., xi.

perspective: one eye is on the foundational traditions of the faith, while the other eye is on the community and its culture, which comprises all the factors that make up the way of life for the people.[7]

In the same way that the common articulation of American history has been little more than white American history, the common articulation of American theology has been little more than white American theology. This is not to say that American history, as it is commonly taught, is wrong; only that it is incomplete insofar as it fails to recognize all who have contributed to the historical record. Consequently, contrary to the ideas of some nascent black theologians, the articulation of *theology* by white males is not inherently wrong. Rather, it is only incomplete insofar as it fails to consider the African-American Christian experience. The black experience provides a perspective for theology in the same vein as it provides a perspective for history. Just as an emphasis on African-American history can enhance and better our understanding of American history, so too does an emphasis on African-American theology enhance and better our understanding of theology. A biblically based and historically consistent black theology will not contradict the historic theology of the church (as the nascent black theologians did). Rather, it will enhance our theological understanding. Such diversity in theology is to the glory of God.

Yet, that raises questions: What does such theology look like in an African-American context? How does one articulate the historic, Reformed tradition from the African-American perspective? How would John Calvin, Martin Luther, or even

---

7. Bruce L. Fields, *Introducing Black Theology: Three Crucial Questions for the Evangelical Church* (Grand Rapids: Baker, 2001), 47.

Jonathan Edwards sound any different in the voice and language of African-Americans? Answers to these questions vary with the persons articulating a theology.

For example, when author and theologian Carl Ellis Jr. wants to discuss the theology of the African-American experience, he relates traditional classic theology to classical music and a biblical black theology to jazz. "Classical theology," according to Ellis, "interacts in critical dialogue with the philosophies of the world. It investigates the attributes of God and communicates primarily through a written tradition. . . . Jazz theology," on the other hand, "is a participation in the basic patterns revealed in biblical life situations. It inquires not only *what* God did and said but *how* he said and did it. . . . The genius of classical theology is in theology *as it was formulated*. . . . The genius of jazz theology is in the theology *as it is done*."[8] Thus when the Scriptures say God's name is "I AM" (Ex. 3:14), Ellis takes the Reformed theology of twentieth-century theologian Cornelius Van Til and contextualizes it to the African-American (jazz theological) language and culture:

> God was saying that his existence is the most obvious and fundamental thing in human experience. There can be no *is* without God's *is*; and since *is* is, God is, because God is is. . . . The only way anyone can declare that God "ain't" is to declare that *is* ain't. And if *is* ain't, there never was a God "ain't" declaration in the first place.[9]

Long before the insights of Ellis, Lemuel Haynes, pastor and theologian in post-revolutionary New England, was

8. Carl F. Ellis Jr., *Free at Last?* (Downers Grove, IL: InterVarsity Press, 1996), 174, his emphasis.
9. Ibid., 158.

contextualizing the brilliant pre-revolutionary Reformed theology of Jonathan Edwards and others. Haynes is known as the first African-American pastor of an all-white American church. From 1788 to 1818 he pastored the Congregational Church in Rutland, Vermont. While faithfully serving in that pulpit, he articulated the biblical, Reformed theological imperatives that he gleaned from the writings of such theological stalwarts as Calvin, Luther, Edwards, and David Brainerd, to name a few.[10] Yet, Haynes did not content himself with merely parroting these great men. He sought to contextualize their theology to the African-American experience of post-revolutionary America, an experience of slavery and bondage in the land of freedom. For Haynes and many of his black intellectual contemporaries, the only biblically faithful approach to this troubling issue was found in the understanding of divine providence so gloriously expressed in Reformed theology. According to a recent biographer,

> Like a number of other eighteenth-century black authors— Jupiter Hammon, James Albert Ukasaw Gronniosaw, Phillis Wheatley, John Marrant, Quobna Ottobah Cugoano, and Olaudau Equiano—Haynes accepted a Calvinistic form of Christianity. Indeed, Calvinism seems to have corroborated the deepest structuring elements of the experience of such men and women as they matured from children living in slavery or servitude into adults desiring freedom, literacy, and membership in a fair society. From Calvinism, this generation of black authors drew a vision of God at work providentially in lives of black people, directing their sufferings yet promising the faithful among them a restoration to his favor and his presence.[11]

10. John Saillant, *Black Puritan, Black Republican: The Life and Thought of Lemuel Haynes* (1753–1833) (New York: Oxford Press, 2003), 91.
11. Ibid., 4.

Haynes was representative of a number of eighteenth-century African-American intellectuals committed to consistent biblical truth.

> Acknowledging the divine providence both of evil and of good, these black Calvinists insisted upon the human obligation to shun sin (which was displayed in the slave trade and slavery) and to further God's benevolent design (which was exemplified in a free and harmonious society). More than any of his peers, black or white, Haynes found in Calvinism a tradition of exegesis that could be leveled against the slave trade and slavery.[12]

Haynes spent most of his theological life promoting and articulating a Calvinistic theology that was biblically faithful, historically consistent, and experientially expressive of African-Americans. To see what Edwards's theological brilliance would look like in an African-American context, we need only to read and understand Lemuel Haynes, who "in applying the logic of the Edwardsean tradition to the situation of African Americans . . . wrote a new chapter into American Calvinism."[13]

Despite obvious God-glorifying benefits of seeking diversity in theology, most of the American theological community has neglected to incorporate the rich theological heritage of her darker brothers and sisters. As a result, it has been diminished to the extent that it has failed to do so. Ironically, though the theological establishment has overlooked the theology of the black experience, black theology is finding a foothold in the church in other ways.

The musical and choral revival that we witnessed in the seventies among charismatic churches and whose fruits are now

12. Ibid.
13. Ibid., 116.

finding an overwhelming acceptance in mainline churches has been largely influenced by the music of the black religious tradition.[14] Many of the songs and choruses of contemporary Christian music are laden with melodies and rhythms that are rooted in Negro spirituals and the blues.[15] Ironically, during the early Christian movement among the slaves, many, particularly with Reformed thinking, frowned upon the music and freedom of expression found in African-American worship. Accordingly,

> Anglicans [and] Presbyterians . . . refused to abide the exuberance the environment of the camp meeting offered to the black community: songs of their own composing, songfests away from proper supervision, and tunes more appropriate for dance rather than for solemn worship.[16]

Charles Colcock Jones was a Presbyterian who, though enthusiastic concerning the mission to the slaves, was less than welcoming of their brand of worship:

> The public worship of God should be conducted with reverence and stillness on the part of the congregation; nor should the minister—whatever may have been the previous habits and training of the people—encourage demonstrations of approbation or disapprobation, or exclamations, or response,

14. This phenomenon is further demonstrated by the rise of urban contemporary music among the white youth of suburban America. Contemporary Christian music is more or less a reflection of the contemporary secular music culture.

15. This is not a new phenomenon. Few American churches at Easter do not incorporate the spiritual "Were You There When They Crucified My Lord?" And the seemingly ubiquitous hymn "Amazing Grace" is believed by some to be sung to the melody of an old slave tune. See "Amazing Grace" (video) with Bill Moyers, produced by Public Broadcasting System.

16. Hatch, *Democratization*, 154.

or noises, or outcries of any kind during the progress of divine worship. . . . One of the great advantages in teaching them [slaves] good Psalms and hymns is that they are thereby induced to lay aside the extravagant and nonsensical chants, and catches and hallelujah songs of their own composing.[17]

Interestingly, what Jones regarded as "nonsensical chants" and "hallelujah songs" has become widespread today in churches denominationally similar to his. Chorus music has found a home among liberal and conservative, traditional and nontraditional churches, as they seek both to reach a new generation and to recapture the celebration of worship found throughout the Bible. In fact, one of the most important contributions that a biblical African-American theological perspective affords may be an understanding of pilgrims' worshiping in a foreign land. Sociologists C. Eric Lincoln and Lawrence H. Mamiya insightfully note that black spirituals offer "a study of how black people 'Africanized' Christianity in America as they sought to find meaning in the turn of events that made them involuntary residents in a strange and hostile land."[18]

SOJOURN AND BLACKNESS

"How shall we sing the Lord's song in a foreign land?"[19] is the rhetorical question asked by the psalmist. It is a question of deep emotive content. It is a question of joy amid times of sorrow, of laughter amid times of tears. It is the cry of a people who must live lives of want and need in a land of plenty. It is the cry of the

17. Quoted in Hatch, *Democratization*, 155.
18. C. Eric Lincoln and Lawrence H. Mamiya, *The Black Church in the African American Experience* (Durham, NC: Duke University Press, 1990), 348.
19. Ps. 137:4.

nation of Israel in exile. And to that extent it is illustrative of the black experience in America. So similar is the analogy, in fact, that one African-American theologian has suggested that like Israel, black Christians, "in the midst of a tragic Diaspora, have acquired a gift of laughter in the midst of tears."[20] By developing a "theology of sorrow and joy,"[21] the nation of Israel gave to the church a paradigm for understanding our pilgrimage through this world—a world in which the Christian is a sojourner in exile awaiting the full restoration found in Jesus Christ. Yet white American Christianity is so far removed from this scenario that it rarely connects with this important motif of the Christian life.

Few among the majority in American Christianity can relate to an experience of exile. Few can relate to having to develop a community gift of laughter in the midst of tears. For Americans have not been conquered or torn from their homeland and expected to sing joyfully of the conquest. This is not to their discredit, but it does hinder their understanding and thus expression of the biblical motif of sojourning. Yet if American theologians were to adopt a perspective of inclusion and not view their theology through myopic lenses, they would see that God has in his sovereignty given to American Christianity a people whose experience of pilgrimage in a foreign land would enrich American faith. How shall we sing the Lord's song in a foreign land? Look to the black Christian experience as an example.

Just as the Psalms often proved invaluable for the Israelites during their most distressful times, so too did the spirituals and

20. J. Deotis Roberts, "Black Theology in the Making," in *Black Theology*, 116.
21. "Sorrow/joy" is an expression coined in reference to the black experience in America. This experience is reflective of a state of oppression that brings about sorrow and a time of deliverance that brings about joy. Though it is used in reflecting on the black experience in America, it is not uniquely black American. Initially it was indicative of the biblical account of Israel's situation in life. Subsequently it has been used by Lerone Bennett and quoted by J. Deotis Roberts (ibid.).

folk songs prove invaluable to the slaves. In fact, as much as anything else, the slaves' songs and spirituals were responsible for the collapse of the slavery system. They were that which maintained hope and bolstered the fortitude of the slaves. The indomitable character of the slaves was instrumental in the ultimate deterioration of slavery, a system based on the dehumanization and degradation of its victims. Singing songs of Zion, songs of hope, invigorated the slaves and reconstituted their resolve to endure until change came.

> The spiritual was the expression of the full range of life experiences garnered by the slave. . . . [The spirituals] were the slave's "sweet consolation and the messages to Heaven, bearing sorrow, pain, joy, prayer and adoration. . . . The man, though a slave, produced the song, and the song in turn produced a better man."[22]

Like the Psalms of Israel, black religion has historically been experiential. It was hewn out of the experiences of a dominated people forced to live on the fringe of an affluent society. And like the Psalms, it grew from the questions about God's presence and seeming apathy toward an oppressed people:

> O God, why have You cast us off forever?
> Why does Your anger smoke against the sheep of Your pasture?
> . . . .
> O God, how long will the adversary reproach?
> Will the enemy blaspheme Your name forever?
> Why do You withdraw Your hand,
>   even Your right hand?

22. Lincoln and Mamiya, *The Black Church in the African American Experience*, 350.

Take it out of Your bosom
 and destroy them. (Ps. 74:1, 10–11)

This song could have been written in ancient Israel, the antebellum South, the turbulent 1960s, or present-day urban America fearing the threat of police brutality and profiling. In fact, only circumstances similar to these can produce such musical pathos. Herein lies the beauty of a biblically based black theological perspective. It is born out of our experiences. It does not speak in the frequently ambiguous terms of traditional theology or in the often-convoluted rhetoric of higher criticism. Rather, it resounds with the expressions of everyday life. It speaks of the joy and pain of being a nation within a nation, of seeing the fruit of your labor but never enjoying the succulent juices of that fruit. Ultimately it preaches and sings about a God who seemingly vanishes in the face of our oppression, yet unmistakably and providentially supplies a table of fulfillment in the presence of our enemies. The roots of this black religious experience are summed up this way by Emmanuel McCall:

> It must be remembered that the substance of the black religious traditions were not fashioned in drawing rooms, theological conferences, ecclesiastical assemblies, cathedrals or seminary campuses. They were hammered out in cotton fields, on plantations, in plantation shanties, in work details and in the obscurity of woods while this servile people attempted to reconcile the divine platitudes mouthed by their masters with the harsh realities of their existence.[23]

23. Emmanuel McCall, "Black Liberation Theology: A Politics of Freedom," *Review and Expositor* 73 (1976): 324.

Today we are afforded the luxuries of theological conferences, ecclesiastical assemblies, and seminary classrooms, yet the need for the church to hammer out her theology in the mundane, everyday existence of people in crisis is as real as ever. Turning theology into practice has been the lot of black Americans since we first set foot on the shores of the New World. Yet the unfortunate circumstances of our sojourn here have actually provided for the good fortune of the church at large.

If the predominantly white church in America desires to know the reality of a providential relationship with God in the midst of oppression as repeatedly demonstrated with ancient Israel, she need only plumb the depths of the rich spiritual heritage of her darker brothers and sisters. There she will not only find the most illustrative analogy of ancient Israel, but also find a people who have struggled with the pain of oppression and often tyrannical forms of discrimination and yet have joyfully witnessed the sustaining hand of God. She will understand that "We Shall Overcome" is not merely wishful platitudes about some future peaceful existence, but simultaneously a powerful testimony to the victories already wrought in our behalf by the hand of God. "We Shall Overcome" says in song what Paul says in Romans 8:28: "that all things work together for good to those who love God, to those who are the called according to His purpose." It is working out for *our* good, and consequently the good of the church as a whole, not simply because we understand the dynamics of the Trinity or the full extent of the atonement, but also because we *love* God and realize that he has called us for his purpose and his glory.

SOVEREIGNTY AND BLACKNESS

As biblical black theologians we cannot help but identify with the existence of blacks in America and the often-debilitating effect that slavery and the subsequent discrimination and segregation have had on black people.[24] Acknowledging this experience, as Reformed theologians we must seek biblically sound answers to the question of African-American history in light of our understanding of God's involvement. For example, in speaking theologically to these concerns, we see that the Bible reveals a God who is sovereign. He is sovereignly in control of human events (Prov. 16:33). He is sovereign over creation (Job 37:6–13; Ps. 104:4; 135:6–7; 148:8). He sovereignly supplies sustenance to the creatures of the field (Job 38:39–41; Ps. 104:27–29; Matt. 6:26; 10:29). He supremely and providentially controls the affairs of nations (Job 12:23; Ps. 22:28; Acts 17:26; 14:16). Ultimately, therefore, he is in control of all aspects of our lives (Job 14:5; Prov. 16:9; 20:24; 21:1; Acts 17:18). Yet this emphasis on the sovereignty of God does not negate the responsibility of humankind and the fact that humans are culpable for their actions (Ezek. 18:4; Rom. 3:23). In seeking to explain the complexity of divine sovereignty and human responsibility, Wayne Grudem usefully draws the analogy of a playwright:

> In the Shakespearean play Macbeth, the character Macbeth murders King Duncan. Now (if we assume for a moment that this is a fictional account), the question may be asked, "Who killed King Duncan?" On one level, the correct answer is "Macbeth." Within the context of the play he carried out the murder and is rightly to blame for it. But on another level, a correct answer to the question, "Who killed King Duncan?" would be "William Shakespeare": he wrote the play, he created the characters in it, and he wrote the part where Macbeth killed King Duncan.

24. As awful as slavery was, Jim Crow may have been even more evil and insidious in its dehumanization and demoralization of black Americans. See Leon T. Witwack, *Trouble in Mind* (New York: Alfred Knopf, 1998).

It would not be correct to say that because Macbeth killed King Duncan, William Shakespeare did not kill him. Nor would it be correct to say that because William Shakespeare killed King Duncan, Macbeth did not kill him. Both are true. On the level of the characters in the play Macbeth fully (100 percent) caused King Duncan's death, but on the level of the creator of the play, William Shakespeare fully (100 percent) caused King Duncan's death. In similar fashion, we can understand that God fully causes things in one way (as Creator), and we fully cause things in another way (as creatures)."[25]

Without a doubt, it is difficult for finite human beings to comprehend the decrees and mind of an infinite God, yet if we are going to be faithful to Scripture we must accept both truths equally. The dynamic interplay between God's sovereignty and human responsibility must always inform our interpretation and understanding of history.

For example, the biblical understanding of God's sovereignty demands acceptance that the kidnapping and subsequent enslavement of Africans in America was according to his eternal and sovereign will. This must never be lost to us as we seek to resolve areas of racial tension and animosity in the church. If God is sovereign, as true sovereignty is biblically defined (see pp. 44–51), then we must acknowledge that it pleased God to bring Africans to the land of America. It pleased him to use the hands and wills of sinful men to do so. This is commonly referred to as God's "hard sovereignty"—hard in the sense that it is difficult for us to grasp and to resolve with our unbalanced sentimental notions of a sweet, loving God. Yet the Bible does not refer to

---

25. Wayne Grudem, *Systematic Theology* (Grand Rapids: Zondervan Publishing, 1994), 321.

God's rule as being "hard" or "soft" but rather as being unquestionably glorious for him and good for us (Rom. 8:28).

Again, the Bible never diminishes God's sovereign control over all things and beings; nor does it skirt the issue of humans' responsibility and culpability for our sinful actions. In fact, much of the unresolved racial and cultural conflict between black and white Christians is founded in a reluctance to see the sovereign hand of God in the slave trade. A biblical understanding would insist that we conclude that the transplanting of Africans to the shores of America was as divinely orchestrated as the pilgrimage of Israel into slavery in Egypt (Gen. 15:13–14) and the migration of the first pilgrims from England to the Plymouth Colony. All are human events over which the Scriptures state that God supremely rules (Prov. 16:33).

Yet even though God ordained that Africans be brought to America in the hollow of slave ships, this in no way absolves the Euro-American establishment of their responsibility for those horrors and subsequent degrading atrocities. This again is graphically illustrated to us by God's not only divinely orchestrating Israel's sojourn into Egypt and ultimately into slavery, but finally judging Egypt with the ten plagues for having subjected the children of Israel to slavery and refusing to set them free (Ex. 7:14–12:36). This event in Scripture is just one of the many indelible reminders that God does not allow the guilty to go unpunished for their lawless deeds (Nah. 1:3), though he sovereignly brings about whatever he desires through the outworking of these deeds. Whereas the rule of God must never be compromised, the culpability of humans likewise must never be diminished. These two concepts, though difficult to reconcile, are held with equal sincerity in the pages of Scripture. And perhaps nowhere are they more closely and succinctly stated than by the apostle Peter in Acts 2:22–24:

> Men of Israel, hear these words: Jesus of Nazareth, a Man attested
> by God to you by miracles, wonders, and signs which God did
> through Him in your midst, as you yourselves also know—Him,
> being delivered by the determined purpose and foreknowledge
> of God, you have taken by lawless hands, have crucified, and
> put to death; whom God raised up, having loosed the pains of
> death, because it was not possible that He should be held by it.

Here Peter is preaching his famous sermon on the day of Pentecost, when the promised Holy Spirit was poured out. In explaining the supernatural occurrences of the day, Peter puts them into a historical context. He speaks of the fulfilling of the words of the prophet Joel and how the coming of Christ and the unprecedented coming of the Holy Spirit were the onset of a new epoch in redemptive history. He then begins to link the event directly to the life and death of Jesus Christ as Messiah. Consequently, Christ's death and those responsible, according to Peter, must be understood on two planes.

First, the deliverance of Christ to the cross and ultimately to death was in accordance with the predetermined plan and knowledge of God (v. 23), since Christ was the "Lamb slain from the foundation of the world" (Rev. 13:8). Peter, in no uncertain terms, affirms the sovereignty of God and his control over even the most horrible of events. He does not seek to absolve God of the responsibility of decreeing the life and subsequent death of Christ. He does not suggest in empty platitudes that God did not do this terrible deed but that he can use it. No, Peter is unmistakably clear. The sinless Son of God was subjected to an unspeakable and humiliating death—crucifixion on a Roman cross—because God determined it to be, and it pleased God to do so (Isa. 53:10).

Second, though God purposed Christ's crucifixion, Peter unequivocally states that the Jewish leaders to whom he was speaking were responsible for committing this lawless act. Those who contrived the arrest and trial of Christ were as culpable for their sin as the soldiers who beat him, spat on him, and drove the nails through his hands. Peter declares that God did not find them guiltless for having so trampled upon his guiltless Son. Indeed, their sin was their sin. Again, it is apparent that the Scriptures never confuse or shy away from the idea of God's sovereignty and human responsibility. Therefore, neither should we.

With this understanding we can confidently say that the large population of blacks in America is certainly in accordance with the predetermined will of God. He ordained our sojourn here. He determined our positions. And he directs our future. Could there be blacks in America had God not wanted it so? Certainly not. Could they have been brought here in chains and sold on the slave block if God had determined to prevent it? Of course not. God never, at any time in the history of the world, stayed his providential hand from the affairs of this life. Even those events that prove themselves most distasteful to us he providentially orders according to his good pleasure. For God has a purpose. God has a plan more glorious than our temporary comforts, as expressed in the poetry of William Cowper:

> Judge not the Lord by feeble sense
> But trust Him for His grace;
> Behind a frowning providence
> He hides a smiling face.[26]

With this in mind, the large extent to which the African-American populace identifies itself as Christian should not be thought coincidental. The predominantly African-American

26. "God moves in a mysterious way."

church is secondarily a testament to the evangelistic zeal of many white American Christians and primarily the divine orchestration of God. In fact, it should be argued that in orchestrating such events, God has providentially designed the re-Africanization of Christianity.[27]

Christianity today is largely thought of as a Western religion. Most around the world associate Christianity with Western civilization, which is driven primarily by the Euro-American cultural expression. In most countries today, to be thought of as American is to be thought of as Christian. And though Christianity is a world religion, having more adherents in more countries than any other faith, to see Christianity portrayed through the American media or in foreign terms is to see a white Euro-American face. Though this may be the general perception today, however, it was not so in the beginning. Christianity at its roots was a religion of color.

Again, on the day of Pentecost, we are given a glimpse of the diversity that the Spirit of God came to unite. Those gathered at Pentecost were from a cross section of peoples, each having a unique language and cultural identity. For those who were gathered in Jerusalem and upon whom the Holy Spirit fell were Jews "from every nation under heaven" (Acts 2:5). In fact, to the amazement of all, with their many diverse cultural expressions and languages, they were miraculously able to hear the apostles (Galileans) in their own native tongues even though they were from various nations:

Parthians and Medes and Elamites, those dwelling in Mesopotamia, Judea and Cappadocia, Pontus and Asia, Phrygia and

27. Lincoln and Mamiya make reference to the "Africanization" of Christianity in America by the songs of the black Christians (*The Black Church in the African American Experience*, 348). Yet the Africanization of Christianity in America is a reflection of the broader notion of the "re-Africanization" of Christianity.

> Pamphylia, Egypt and the parts of Libya adjoining Cyrene, visitors from Rome, both Jews and proselytes, Cretans and Arabs. . . . (Acts 2:9–11)

Even a surface understanding of this text reveals an undeniable diversity and the intention of God to build a church of various cultural and racial backgrounds. Not only was the ethnic makeup of the early church diverse (many prominent components being of African descent), but the cultural expression of early Christianity in its worship forms reflected this diversity as well.

Rooted in the Middle East, Christianity initially took hold among those who displayed a wide range of skin complexion. The early spread of the gospel into the African continent produced many leaders who are even now held in high esteem. According to Glen Usry and Craig Keener:

> Even in the nineteenth century, European scholar Theodor Mommsen acknowledged that "through Africa Christianity became the religion of the world." Nearly half of the most prominent church leaders in the first few centuries (such as Origen, Cyprian, Athanasius, and Augustine) were North African, and probably a fair number of these were dark in complexion.[28]

In fact, an examination of the writings of the renowned church father, Augustine of Hippo, the great Archbishop of Carthage in Northern Africa, reveals a worship form indicative of the prominent form in today's African-American church. According to Augustine's testimony of his church service in which a young man was miraculously healed:

28. Glen Usry and Craig Keener, *Black Man's Religion* (Downers Grove, IL: InterVarsity Press, 1996), 33. See also Mark Shaw, *Kingdom of God in Africa* (Grand Rapids: Baker, 1996), 41–72.

And lo, he arose, and was not shaking, for he was healed, and stood there well, looking at them as they looked at him. So who could refrain from praising God? *The whole church was filled with cries of joy and thanksgiving.* Then people ran to me where I was sitting, just ready to enter the church. One after another they came in, each arrival announcing as news what another had already told me. While I was rejoicing and silently thanking God the man himself came in with several others and knelt at my knees. I raised him up and kissed him, and we went in to the people. *The church was full and was echoing with shouts of joy. No one was silent, but on this side and on that they were crying, "God be thanked," and "God be praised." I greeted the people, and they cried out as before, and even more fervently.* When at last there was silence, the appointed portions of the sacred writings were read. But when the time for my sermon came, I made only a few remarks appropriate to the time and the joy of that rejoicing. For I preferred to let them ponder the eloquence, so to speak, of God as he declared himself through his divine action instead of hearing about it.[29]

Without any liturgical connection or any direct historical lineage, Augustine's description of a worship service in which he preached could easily and accurately be a description of a worship service in many National Baptist, African Methodist Episcopal, Church of God in Christ, and other predominantly African-American churches today.

Nevertheless, despite Christianity's early Middle Eastern and African influences, by the Middle Ages Christianity was finding its most prominent expression in Europe. The cultural associations

---

29. Augustine, *City of God: Against the Pagans*, vol. 7, trans. William M. Green (Cambridge, MA: Harvard University Press, 1972), 247.

were primarily European, and when Europeans began exploration into the New World, the Christianity that accompanied them was distinctly European. Subsequently, the forced migration of Africans to continental America and their resultant introduction to this Christianity was in effect the re-Africanization of Christianity. In a real and legitimate sense, Africa gave Christianity to the Europeans, the Europeans gave Christianity to America, and America was now once again giving Christianity back to Africa. Not to see the providential hand of God in this cycle is to ignore the reality of God working in and through history.

Yet some will ask, "Did this providence of God have to be worked out on the bruised and battered backs of African men and women? Did they have to bear the brunt of his bitter rod, that his purposes be revealed? Did white America have to experience the debilitating and insidious moral corruption inherent in thoughts and actions of racial superiority that God's purposes might stand?" Who could know why God's providence had to be so bitter? Who could venture to explain God's ways of infinite knowledge, unsearchable wisdom, and unfathomable mercy? Though he does not reconcile all things, the poet William Cowper does put our minds in the right frame when he writes:

> His purpose will ripen fast,
> Unfolding every hour;
> The bud may have a bitter taste,
> But sweet will be the flower.
>
> Blind unbelief is sure to err,
> And scan his work in vain;
> God is his own interpreter,
> And he will make it plain.

And one of the glorious results of this providential work of God has been the establishing of one of the most stable institutions in Western civilization, the predominantly African-American church. Indeed, it stands as the most visible demonstration of God's sovereignty, humankind's sinfulness, and Christ's sufficiency. It stands as a glorious monument to his bittersweet providence.

Nonetheless, in spite of this glorious result, we must not neglect the responsibility of humans in the travesties that accompanied this re-Africanization. Again, the lawless acts associated with racism and discrimination that accompanied the Middle Passage[30] and the institution of slavery in America are the sins of primarily white Euro-America. Just as Egyptians were culpable and judged for enslaving the Israelites, though God had ordained it to be, America, often with the condoning rhetoric of the church, is culpable for its part in the enslavement of Africans and has been and is being judged for it. Until we as biblical theologians, white and black, grapple with the sovereignty of God, the sinfulness of humans, and the all-sufficient work of Christ in the reconciliation of the races in America, we will not progress far along the road to racial harmony outside or, even more importantly, inside the church.

> Father, our Father, we bend our knees to your will. Grant that we in our pain may know you in your power. For we know that it is in our submitting that we are used. And it is through our suffering that you are glorified. For our temporary affliction is indeed working out for us a greater weight of glory. May we

30. The route taken by slave ships from the west coast of Africa to North and South America during the Atlantic slave trade. Along this route lie the dead corpses of untold thousands of African men, women, and children who did not survive the cruel and inhumane conditions of the voyage.

find comfort in that our eyes are not yet ready to behold such glory and our hearts are not yet tuned for such praise. Father, continue to mold us and purge us, even by fire, that we may be prepared to share in your majesty. The days of our sojourn often drag long, and hope can find itself deferred. But Lord, we pray to remain steadfast. We pray to rest each evening in a hope secure. We pray to keep our eyes on our Blessed Hope—knowing that whether this world comes or goes, our Hope springs eternal.

Discussion Questions

1. Predestination is a biblical doctrine (Eph. 1:5), yet many find it troublesome. Why is this? How would you answer their objections?
2. In what ways does diversity in theology help us understand God and each other better?
3. In what ways does theology from African-American experience help us to know the God of the Bible better? What Psalms might give us insight into this question?
4. What is meant by the "re-Africanization" of Christianity?
5. What was the approach of Lemuel Haynes and other 18th century black intellectuals to slavery in America? How might their approach give us some perspective in addressing issues of injustice in our day?

FIVE

Embracing the Truth

I don't feel no ways tired;
I've come too far from where I started from.
Nobody told me the road would be easy.
I don't believe He brought me this far to leave me.
—black gospel song

I stated in the beginning of this book that seminary was great. It exposed me to some of the most acute and adroit theological minds the Christian world has to offer. Yet, besides the indispensable theological education I received, the greatest lesson I learned at seminary is the one I have tried to communicate in these pages: One does not have to stop being African American in order to be Reformed. While this may seem obvious to many in the majority culture, it nevertheless is a message that needs to be communicated clearly and without horns.

Our white brothers and sisters need to know that many, indeed most, African Americans struggle with maintaining their cultural distinctiveness while fully embracing the truths of Reformed theology. And African-American Christians should be assured that their experience is not a stumbling block to embracing the truths of the Reformation, but rather a stepping-stone.

Why should African Americans embrace a Reformed theological understanding? Because like any segment of the church, African-American Christians should see their experience and existence as being ordained by God, according to his plan and for his glory. We should eagerly embrace Reformed theology because it aligns with everything that the African-American church has sought to be: biblical, historical, and experiential. Reformed theology brings these three pillars of truth together more consistently than any other.

Biblical

Since its inception, the predominantly African-American church has held the Bible in the highest regard. The Bible has been the center of community as well as church life. The most prominent leaders within the African-American community have been men and women of the church. Their oratorical legacy is one laced with biblical references and theological language. In light of that, the Reformed commitment to the Bible as the primary source of truth and authority should find a warm welcome in African-American Christianity.

Reformed theology has long been a stalwart in the defense of the integrity of the Bible. From the Reformation's chief article *sola Scriptura* (Scripture alone), to the clarity of the Reformed confessions and catechisms, to the more recent Chicago Statement on Biblical Inerrancy, reformation thought and theologians have led the way in maintaining the Bible's integrity. With such a high regard for Scripture, it is not coincidental that Reformed theology insists upon a clearly biblical, logical, and systematic approach to theology.

Historical

If anything has distinguished the predominantly African-American church, it has been its remarkable and commendable insistence on remembering and honoring those who have gone before. The plethora of special days and anniversaries we find throughout African-American churches is a testament to its desire to maintain an unbroken connection with its past. Such an insistence is to be commended for its glorious recognition that we do not stand alone. And such an insistence would be right at home in Reformed theology.

Reformed theology, besides being biblical, is consciously historical. The Reformed tradition has always sought to ground its theology in the great teachings of the history of the church. If we do theology without reference to history, the danger of going beyond revealed biblical truth always lurks just outside the door of our study. Reformed theology understands that while we are always seeking new expressions of the truth, we are not seeking new truth.

Experiential

As we have demonstrated in the preceding pages, the predominantly African-American church is unapologetically experiential. The life and tenor of the African-American church has been one not simply of talking about the faith, but also of living out that faith. It has rarely been interested in theological pontification without practical application. This truth is found in the songs and spirituals, many of which blended theology and life (though often with more life than theology). Life was never to be understood apart from the knowledge of God and his providential care. Yet, God was never to be contemplated apart from his everyday and intimate connection to the life he gave. In this too, African Americans can find a home and a platform in the Reformed theological tradition.

Reformed theology, properly understood, is inherently experiential. It corresponds to reality and the experience of humans in their relationships with each other and with God. From the doctrine of sin to the doctrine of glorification, theology that is out of touch with human experience is a theology not worth holding. A proper understanding of our experiences will be consistently expounded in the Scriptures and will be collaborated by analogous experiences of men and women throughout the history of the church. Reformed theology sees all of life, every experience, as being within the sovereign plan and purpose of God and thus for his glory and our good.

All three of these categories are important if we are going to articulate and sustain a glory-saturated, God-focused theology. How these three relate to one another is obvious. The priority of the categories can be set with this simple maxim: Cautiously go against experience; rarely go against history; and never go against the Bible. Hold firmly to Reformed teaching, and while there is plenty of wiggle room for theorizing on the implications of scriptural theology, you will be safe within the boundaries of the Bible, history, and experience.

Finally, the issue may be summed up with two questions: Can African Americans be Reformed? Yes. The truth of God's matchless grace crosses over all cultural and racial boundaries. The eternal truths recovered during the Reformation should in no way be limited to any cultural expression and race of people. In fact, the Reformation will only be complete once the elect from every tongue, tribe, and nation have embraced these truths.

Should African Americans be Reformed? Again, yes. Reformed theology is biblical, historical, and experiential. African Americans have had no difficulty in locating these three pillars of truth in their sojourn and should seek to fully incorporate them in their quest for God. We can be Reformed because, contrary to popular opinion, we do not have to stop being African American to do so. God created us the way we are, as he created all the peoples of the earth to give expression to his glory and grace according to the truth he has revealed. We can, indeed we must, seek to understand our calling not apart from how he has created us, but in light of how he has created us. And whether it is in preaching, praising, or praying we will do it all to the glory of God. Amen.

Father, just as the cries of Israel went up before you, and you were moved to show yourself strong in their behalf, our cries too do now go up to you, seeking your salvation in our midst. There is nothing we accomplish unless you accomplish it through us. There is no power we display unless it is your power through us. For the weakness of this your people is the strength of you, their God. The foolishness of this your people is the wisdom of you, their God. Do Lord, be our strength and our wisdom. Let us not trust in the power of our legs or the skillfulness of our tongues, but let us trust in this—namely, that we are your people and you know those who are your own; and you are relentless in bestowing upon them goodness and mercy, wisdom and strength.

Discussion Questions

1. Is Reformed theology compatible with the African-American experience?
2. Why should African-Americans embrace Reformed Theology?
3. What can the broader church learn from the experience of African-American Christianity?

Limping Toward Reconciliation

My high school football coach was a man of integrity and Christian principle. When he spoke, people listened because his life backed his words. It is no wonder that many of those lessons he taught us are still with me today. One of those lessons was the result of his years of growing up in a time of racial unrest.

As a young boy he was well schooled in the ways of discrimination. He lived it during most of his maturing years. He saw firsthand how a society fraught with discriminatory practices and segregation laws could castrate a man's ability and desire to function as a man. He observed a system devised to keep black men politically, socially, and psychologically impotent. He witnessed the futility of the black man's attempts to make a substantial contribution to societal structure because of that oppressive system. Like any young man of his day, he was frustrated by the insidiousness of racism. By the grace of God, he was able to come out of the system, seemingly devised to keep him down, with a degree in education and the recognized ability to lead men. But many of his contemporaries were not as fortunate.

Years later, when he assumed the position of one who had influence on young black minds, he would use every opportunity to influence those minds toward Christ and black awareness. I fondly recall one of those occurrences in which he explained to me the dynamics of the oppressor and the oppressed. In his insightful and amicable way, he taught me to look at the cause, not just the result. In other words, he said, if a man is limping with a cane, don't sit there and mock or criticize him; rather, find out the cause of the limp and see if sympathy is warranted. With this illustration, he would go on to make the correlation between white and black America.

For him, the black man was viewed by white America as limping around with a cane because black America was given over to complaining about social conditions, lack of employment opportunities, economic constraint, political impotence, racism, and discrimination. But the limp was all that most of white America could see. Coach, however, told me that to whatever degree black America was limping through its existence, it was due in large part to the fact that someone had kicked it. And as he put it, "It is not right to kick a man and then complain that the man has a limp." Sadly, however, this is what many in America have done. Even sadder is that many in the church have done the same thing.

Segregation in the church can be analogized to a limp. It is a disability in the body of Christ that everyone sees, that everyone abhors, but that few within the conservative evangelical church have been willing to address. That is, until the glorious reports of recent times. It seems that the evangelical church in America is finally realizing that the limp that is segregation and discrimination in our pews and pulpits is due in large part to white Christians' having kicked black Christians at a time in the history of the American church when open arms should have been the order of the day. Nevertheless, the limping is becoming less pronounced.

In recent times, three of the most prominent, predominantly white, conservative denominations in America have made public confessions and resolutions concerning their involvement in the volatile racial climate of American history and the regrettable, duplicitous way in which they related to their brothers and sisters of African descent. Realizing that slavery, Jim Crow, and subsequent discrimination experienced by blacks in America was empowered by churches that are part of the historical lineage of these present-day denominations, these communions have denounced the sins of their fathers and resolved to confront racism and discrimination wherever it may be found. Knowing that reconciliation begins only after transgressions have been admitted, the Assemblies of God (AG), the Southern Baptist Convention (SBC), and the Presbyterian Church in America (PCA) have made substantial and significant statements concerning the racism that mars their pasts and the reconciliation they pray will define their futures. These are important statements in the history of the American church. And while they do not wipe away the effects of so many years of racism and discrimination, they do give us hope that one day we will be able to stride hand in hand into worship—with no distracting canes.

ASSEMBLIES OF GOD

In October 1994, in Memphis, Tennessee, the Assemblies of God, along with several other predominantly white Pentecostal denominations, met with representatives from the predominantly black Pentecostal denomination the Church of God in Christ (COGIC) and repented of their sins against their black Pentecostal brothers and sisters. In fact, the large all-white Pentecostal umbrella organization known as Pentecostal Fellowship of North America (PFNA), founded in 1948, was dissolved and a new umbrella organization that included both black and white Pentecostal groups was formed: Pentecostals and Charismatic Churches of North America (PCCNA). This landmark event, which many refer to as the "Miracle in Memphis," produced what the PCCNA calls the *Racial Reconciliation Manifesto*. It states:

> Challenged by the reality of our racial divisions, we have been drawn by the Holy Spirit to Memphis, Tennessee, October 17–19, 1994 in order to become true "Pentecostal Partners" and to develop together "A Reconciliation Strategy for 21st Century Ministry." We desire to covenant together in the ongoing task of racial reconciliation by committing ourselves to the following agenda.

> I. I pledge in concert with my brothers and sisters of many hues to oppose racism prophetically in all its various manifestations within and without the Body of Christ and to be vigilant in the struggle with all my God-given might.

> II. I am committed personally to treat those in the Fellowship who are not of my race or ethnicity, regardless of color, with love and respect as my sisters and brothers in Christ. I am further committed to work against all forms of personal and institutional racism, including those which are revealed within the very structures of our environment.

> III. With complete bold and courageous honesty, we mutually confess that racism is sin and as a blight in the Fellowship must be condemned for having hindered the maturation of spiritual development and mutual sharing among Pentecostal-Charismatic believers for decades.

IV. We openly confess our shortcomings and our participation in the sin of racism by our silence, denial and blindness. We admit the harm it has brought to generations born and unborn. We strongly contend that the past does not always completely determine the future. New horizons are emerging. God wants to do a new thing through His people.

V. We admit that there is no single solution to racism in the Fellowship. We pray and are open to tough love and radical repentance with deep sensitivity to the Holy Spirit as Liberator.

VI. Together we will work to affirm one another's strengths and acknowledge our own weaknesses and inadequacies, recognizing that all of us only "see in a mirror dimly" what God desires to do in this world. Together, we affirm the wholeness of the Body of Christ as fully inclusive of Christians regardless of color. We, therefore, commit ourselves "to love one another with mutual affection, outdoing one another in showing honor" (Romans 12:10).

VII. We commit ourselves not only to pray but also to work for genuine and visible manifestations of Christian unity.

VIII. We hereby commit ourselves not only to the task of making prophetic denouncement of racism in word and creed, but to live by acting in deed. We will fully support and encourage those among us who are attempting change.

IX. We pledge that we will return to our various constituencies and appeal to them for logistical support and intervention as necessary in opposing racism. We will seek partnerships and exchange pulpits with persons of a different hue, not in a paternalistic sense, but in the Spirit of our Blessed Lord who prayed that we might be one (John 17:21).

X. We commit ourselves to leaving our comfort zones, lay aside our warring, racial allegiances, respecting the full humanity of all, live with an openness to authentic liberation which is a product of Divine Creation, until the shackles fall and all bondage ceases.

XI. At the beginning of the twentieth century, the Azusa Street Mission was a model of preaching and living the Gospel message in the world. We desire to drink deeply from the well of Pentecost as it was embodied in that mission. We, therefore, pledge our commitment to embrace the essential commitments of that mission in evangelism and mission, in justice and holiness, in spiritual renewal and empowerment, and in the reconciliation of all Christians regardless of race or gender as we move into the new millennium.[1]

SOUTHERN BAPTIST CONVENTION

In June 1995, the largest Protestant denomination in the world, the Southern Baptist Convention, met in Atlanta, Georgia, for its 150th anniversary. There it was resolved that the Southern Baptist Convention would make a public statement confessing the sins of its past and making fresh commitments to its future as a denomination committed to the gospel of peace and to racial and ethnic reconciliation. The *Resolution on Racial Reconciliation on the 150th Anniversary of the Southern Baptist Convention* states:

1. The *Racial Reconciliation Manifesto* can be found at http://pctii.org/manifesto.html.

WHEREAS, Since its founding in 1845, the Southern Baptist Convention has been an effective instrument of God in missions, evangelism, and social ministry; and

WHEREAS, The Scriptures teach that Eve is the mother of all living (Genesis 3:20), and that God shows no partiality, but in every nation whoever fears him and works righteousness is accepted by him (Acts 10:34–35), and that God has made from one blood every nation of men to dwell on the face of the earth (Acts 17:26); and

WHEREAS, Our relationship to African-Americans has been hindered from the beginning by the role that slavery played in the formation of the Southern Baptist Convention; and

WHEREAS, Many of our Southern Baptist forebears defended the right to own slaves, and either participated in, supported, or acquiesced in the particularly inhumane nature of American slavery; and

WHEREAS, In later years Southern Baptists failed, in many cases, to support, and in some cases opposed, legitimate initiatives to secure the civil rights of African-Americans; and

WHEREAS, Racism has led to discrimination, oppression, injustice, and violence, both in the Civil War and throughout the history of our nation; and

WHEREAS, Racism has divided the body of Christ and Southern Baptists in particular, and separated us from our African-American brothers and sisters; and

WHEREAS, Many of our congregations have intentionally and/or unintentionally excluded African-Americans from worship, membership, and leadership; and

WHEREAS, Racism profoundly distorts our understanding of Christian morality, leading some Southern Baptists to believe that racial prejudice and discrimination are compatible with the Gospel; and

WHEREAS, Jesus performed the ministry of reconciliation to restore sinners to a right relationship with the Heavenly Father, and to establish right relations among all human beings, especially within the family of faith.

Therefore, be it RESOLVED, That we, the messengers to the Sesquicentennial meeting of the Southern Baptist Convention, assembled in Atlanta, Georgia, June 20–22, 1995, unwaveringly denounce racism, in all its forms, as deplorable sin; and

Be it further RESOLVED, That we affirm the Bible's teaching that every human life is sacred, and is of equal and immeasurable worth, made in God's image, regardless of race or ethnicity (Genesis 1:27), and that, with respect to salvation through Christ, there is neither Jew nor Greek, there is neither slave nor free, there is neither male nor female, for (we) are all one in Christ Jesus (Galatians 3:28); and

Be it further RESOLVED, That we lament and repudiate historic acts of evil such as slavery from which we continue to reap a bitter harvest, and we recognize that the racism which yet plagues our culture today is inextricably tied to the past; and

Be it further RESOLVED, That we apologize to all African-Americans for condoning and/or perpetuating individual and systemic racism in our lifetime; and we genuinely repent of racism of which we have been guilty, whether consciously (Psalm 19:13) or unconsciously (Leviticus 4:27); and

Be it further RESOLVED, That we ask forgiveness from our African-American brothers and sisters, acknowledging that our own healing is at stake; and

Be it further RESOLVED, That we hereby commit ourselves to eradicate racism in all its forms from Southern Baptist life and ministry; and

Be it further RESOLVED, That we commit ourselves to be doers of the Word (James 1:22) by pursuing racial reconciliation in all our relationships, especially with our brothers and sisters in Christ (1 John 2:6), to the end that our light would so shine before others, that they may see (our) good works and glorify (our) Father in heaven (Matthew 5:16); and

Be it finally RESOLVED, That we pledge our commitment to the Great Commission task of making disciples of all people (Matthew 28:19), confessing that in the church God is calling together one people from every tribe and nation (Revelation 5:9), and proclaiming that the Gospel of our Lord Jesus Christ is the only certain and sufficient ground upon which redeemed persons will stand together in restored family union as joint-heirs with Christ (Romans 8:17).[2]

2. The *Resolution on Racial Reconciliation on the 150th Anniversary of the Southern Baptist Convention* can be found at http://sbc.net/resolutions/amResolution.asp?ID=899.

Presbyterian Church in America

In June 2002, at the 30th General Assembly of the Presbyterian Church in America, the Nashville Presbytery sponsored an overture calling for a church-wide condemnation of the institution of American slavery and repentance of a heritage that had participated in and failed to denounce the institution and its subsequent discrimination. Though the overture sparked much debate, it was overwhelmingly passed as the PCA moved into a greater understanding of its calling as a Christian witness to the nations. *Overture 20 on Racial Reconciliation* states:

1. Whereas, the Scriptures portray a covenantal pattern of both celebration of our rich heritage and repentance for the sins of our fathers; and,

2. Whereas, our nation has been blessed even as we have repeatedly addressed iniquity, redressed injustice, and assessed restitution for our inconsistent application of the ideals of truth and freedom; and,

3. Whereas, the heinous sins attendant with unbiblical forms of servitude—including oppression, racism, exploitation, manstealing, and chattel slavery—remain among the defining features of our national history; and,

4. Whereas, the issues surrounding that part of our history continue to shape our national life, even creating barriers between brothers and sisters of different races and/or economic spheres from enjoying unencumbered Christian fellowship with one another; and,

128

5. Whereas, the aftereffects of that part of our history continue to be felt in the economic, cultural, and social affairs of the communities in which we live and minister;

We therefore confess our covenantal involvement in these national sins. As a people, both we and our fathers, have failed to keep the commandments, the statutes, and the laws our God has commanded. We therefore publicly repent of our pride, our complacency, and our complicity. Furthermore, we seek the forgiveness of our brothers and sisters for the reticence of our hearts which has constrained us from acting swiftly in this matter.

As a people, we pledge to work hard, in a manner consistent with the Gospel imperatives, for the encouragement of racial reconciliation, the establishment of urban and minority congregations, and the enhancement of existing ministries of mercy in our cities, among the poor, and across all social, racial, and economic boundaries, to the glory of God. Amen.[3]

---

3. *Overture 20 of the Presbyterian Church in America 30th General Assembly* can be found at http://pcahistory.org/pca/race.html.

Connecting to the Historical Faith

This message was delivered at the 2001 African-American Pastors Conference sponsored by the Alliance of Confessing Evangelicals held in Miami, Florida, at Glendale Baptist Church. The message was entitled "The Faith Once Delivered." The object of this discourse is to show the necessity and even preference of understanding and articulating Christianity not only within a biblical framework but within a historical framework as well.

The disconnect that exists between black Christians and white Christians in America can be traced to our lack of understanding of the historical commonality that exists between these two groups. In order to bridge this divide, blacks must study the history of the church and see how their beliefs are rooted in the historical truths of the faith. Also, whites must study the history of the church, particularly as it has been developed among African Americans, to see just how similarly God has worked in the midst of both groups to bring out the truths we hold so dear. The purpose of this lecture was to do just that. It was to show the need for African Americans, in particular, to ground their scriptural understanding in the historical truths handed down through the church by the Holy Spirit without necessarily losing their cultural distinctive.

* * *

Beloved, while I was very diligent to write to you
concerning our common salvation, I found it necessary
to write to you exhorting you to contend earnestly for the faith
which was once for all delivered to the saints.
—Jude 3

On Sunday, April 13, 1997, golf came of age. It was catapulted from the back page to the front page. It stepped out of the shadows of its less modest sporting cousins (football, baseball, basketball, hockey) and into the spotlight of center stage of the American athletic mainstream. It was the day that Tiger Woods became a social icon. It was the day that Tiger Woods became the first African American to win the Masters.

With his triumph, Tiger did not simply open the door to America's favorite white elitist sport, but he more accurately knocked the walls down. An African American winning the Masters would have been story enough. But Tiger did not just win the event; he won in record fashion. In securing his victory, Tiger set 20 Masters records, including lowest tournament score (270, 18 under par), youngest champion (21 years old), widest margin of victory (12 strokes), and tied six others.[1] Augusta National

---

1. For a complete listing of Tiger's Masters records, see *1998 Masters Journal* (Augusta National Golf Club [1998]), 43.

Golf Club, once the symbol of white Southern aristocracy, was this day all abuzz with the glowing smile and uncommon charisma of its first African-American champion, who was but the tender age of 21. The question most were asking was not could he win again, but how many times would he win? None other than Jack Nicklaus himself declared that Tiger would win at least ten. Unimaginable! Until now.

While others were grasping for the words to describe what Tiger had accomplished, Tiger knew what he had done. He could see it on the stunned faces of the Augusta National members. He could hear it in the whispers of the African-American cooks, stewards, and groundskeepers. He knew that this was a historic moment.

On that Sunday, as Tiger made his way out of the locker room and back onto the putting green for the trophy presentation, an entourage of television personalities, reporters, friends, and family closely walked with him. Suddenly Tiger out of the corner of his eye noticed an elderly, dark-skinned, graying gentleman. Tiger halted and said to those with him, "Wait." He looked out at the gentleman and said, "Lee, come here." As the two of them embraced, Tiger whispered in the old man's ear, "Thanks for making this possible." There was Tiger Woods, the first African American to win the Masters, embracing and thanking Lee Elder, the first African American to play in the Masters.

Tiger had a sense of history. As he strolled to receive his trophy and first-place prize money, he knew that he did what he did because men like Lee Elder, Charlie Sifford, Teddy Rhodes, and others did what they did.[2] He knew he stood where he stood

2. For a detailed history of African Americans in the history of golf, see Pete McDaniel, *Uneven Lies* (The American Golfer, 2000).

because men like these stood where they stood. If Tiger Woods is the greatest golfer this world has ever known, one of the reasons is that he understands the history of the game.

Today, if Christianity is, as I contend, miles wide but only inches deep, it is because we have a generation of Christians who do not understand the history of the game. We have a modern church composed of Christians whose understanding of the faith does not extend any further than today's newspaper, latest Christian fad, or popular bestseller. This is illustrated by the seemingly insatiable need for today's Christian community to invent everything "Christian."

Like no Christian generation before, today we have everything "Christian." Every form of entertainment and faddish behavior and thinking the world has developed, the church has devised the "Christian alternative." To this end, Christianity stretches from coast to coast and has its tentacles into every known arena, whether it belongs or not. There seemingly is no sphere of entertainment or behavior in which Christians have not sought to capitalize upon the popularity of that thing. There is the lucrative Christian rock and rap music, Christian movies, talk shows, radio, amusement parks, nightclubs, and proms. As outrageous as it may seem, there is now a group in Texas who have established what they are referring to as the Christian Wrestling Federation (CWF), the Christian alternative to the increasingly popular World Wrestling Federation (WWF). The CWF claims to be "your alternative outreach ministry, professional wrestling with a message."[3]

3. The website where this quotation is located is http://www.christianwrestling.com. [The vision statement has since been updated: "To be a Christian outreach ministry that shares the love of Jesus Christ, through wrestling events around the world" ("Our Mission," Christian Wrestling Foundation, accessed December 22, 2015, http://www.christianwrestling.com/about-2/).]

In assessing the mindless assimilation of modern Christianity to the world's formulas, John MacArthur states:

> There seems almost no limit to what modern church leaders will do to entice people who aren't interested in worship and preaching. Too many have bought the notion that the church must win people by offering an alternative form of entertainment.
>
> Just how far will the church go in competing with Hollywood? A large church in the southwestern United States has installed a half-million dollar special effects system that can produce smoke, fire, sparks, and laser lights in the auditorium. The church sent staff members to study live special effects at Bally's Casino in Las Vegas.[4]

These and other shenanigans, though offered to the church as the Christian "unique and alternative outreach," are nothing more than the inadequate and unimaginative thinking on the part of this Christian generation.

It was Os Guinness who accurately described this generation of Christians as having "fit bodies but fat minds." He states:

> American evangelicals in the last generation have simultaneously toned up their bodies and dumbed down their minds. The result? Many suffer from a modern form of what the ancient Stoics called "mental hedonism"—having fit bodies but fat minds.[5]

We have lost our willingness, and subsequently our ability, to think. The noted twentieth-century philosopher Bertrand Russell

4. John F. MacArthur, *Ashamed of the Gospel* (Wheaton, IL: Crossway, 1999), 70.
5. Os Guinness, *Fit Bodies Fat Minds* (Grand Rapids: Baker, 1994), 10.

suggested that most Christians would rather die than think—and in fact do. Though many Christians congratulate each other on the ubiquitous nature of Christianity in their culture (more accurately vice versa), ironically the one thing Christian we don't have is what we need most—a Christian mind.

Thinking Christians today are actually frowned upon. Biblical thinking is foreign to most in the pew primarily because it is foreign to most in the pulpit. In fact, there is a cancerous surge in modern Christianity toward the anti-intellectual. This anti-intellectualism is producing spiritually inept followers. Though it is conveyed through various means, two particular means are common among African-American Christians: fundamentalism and liberalism.

Fundamentalism, with its legalistic and moralistic preaching, conveys an anti-intellectualism that says "just me and my Bible" (usually King James only). It spurns serious theological reflection or historical insight. Rather, it holds to the spurious and fallacious notion of "no creed but Christ." It is fond of referring to seminaries as cemeteries.

Liberalism is also fertile ground for anti-intellectualism. Though priding itself on being intellectually enlightened, actually and ironically, it is more anti-intellectual. It has declared the Bible culturally irrelevant. Thinking theologically is not encouraged. Rather, the emphasis is upon social action and political preaching. The sermons that inform this movement are not theologically based or historically grounded but are calls to social action and economic reform. Os Guinness summed up this trend by emphasizing the effect this brand of pluralism has had on evangelicalism, particularly with its emphasis on "deeds over creeds."[6] Thus, with its focus on social movements and political

6. Ibid., 53.

agendas, liberalism, like fundamentalism, too has pews full of the spiritually starved and malnourished.

At the heart of this anti-intellectualism, on both the liberal and fundamental fronts, is a blatant disregard for the historicity of the Christian faith. The fundamentalists see issues of history and tradition as biblically irrelevant and the unwarranted products of human reasoning. The liberals see issues of history not so much as unwarranted products of human reasoning, but as culturally confined and therefore socially irrelevant. This disregard has led to a popular Christianity where repentance is nothing more than recovery; holiness is the product of human effort either by abstaining from certain vices (alcohol, tobacco, etc.) or by voting and advocating the correct political platform. The insidious nature of this anti-intellectualism cannot be overstated and must not be understated. David Wells, in his analysis of the modern evangelical mind, suggests as much:

> The stakes are high: the anti-theological mood that now grips the evangelical world is changing its eternal configuration, its effectiveness, and its relation to the past. It is severing the link to historical, Protestant orthodoxy.[7]

It has also produced a church of isolationists. The majority of Christians see their faith as personal and private. The gospel has been swallowed up by a generation consumed with the "me" and the "now." Much of the church considers itself "free of all philosophical frameworks and any historical shaping of their faith and thinking."[8] Without any framework or historical parameters, this popular brand of Christianity has

---

7. David Wells, *No Place for Truth* (Grand Rapids: Eerdmans, 1993), 96.
8. Guinness, *Fit Bodies*, 46.

devolved Christian worship into a human entertainment event and the sermon into a mass counseling session, void of any of the critical thinking concerning the historical doctrines of the Christian faith (God, sin, man, atonement, etc.). While this neglect of history is a tragedy of eternal significance throughout the Christian church, it is especially surprising among African Americans.

African Americans are historically minded people. We are given to historical reflection. Most African Americans can recall the first African American to be a Supreme Court justice, play major-league baseball, perform blood transfusions, and so on. In fact, these facts become sources of pride as we pass along the significance of these people and events to the subsequent generations through the plethora of African-American history celebrations. Unfortunately, our deftness at African-American history is not demonstrated in our understanding of church history. While the average African-American Christian can tell the impact of Martin Luther King, most would be lost in articulating the significance of Martin Luther.

It was Carter Woodson, the preeminent African-American historian, who said, "History is a record of the progress of mankind rather than racial or national achievements." Similarly, history for the Christian must not be simply the recounting of individual achievements by an elite few in their area of expertise whereby we identify the first in a particular race to accomplish certain things. History for the Christian is catholic. That is, it is universal. It is the realization of the progress of redemption whereby God is unfolding the revelation of his kingdom in time and space. And we realize that he is bringing about this revelation through the lives of men and women from every tongue, tribe, and nation. Consequently, the history of redemption is not black history, white history, or brown history. It is God's history. And as African Americans and Euro-Americans we are impoverished if we do not see that we have a common heritage. From Martin Luther to Martin Luther King we all are present in the history of redemption and therefore must contend for the historical faith, the faith that has once and for all been delivered to the saints.

Christianity is inherently a historical faith. It is a faith inextricably woven into the fabric of history. Christianity does not make fanciful, mystical assertions that stand outside of history, but rather is founded upon the truth of God that is established in history. Our God is a God who is in and over history. He is in history in that he has revealed himself in space and time through the historical person of Jesus Christ. Yet he is over history because his existence is without beginning and without end. All things exist and are kept in existence because of the only self-existing One. He rules over and sovereignly dictates the course of history and "brings about whatsoever comes to pass."[9]

Therefore, our sermons and our songs should reflect our understanding of our Christian history. Unfortunately, most sermons today make little or no reference to the historicity of Christianity. Most have little use for the wisdom of the Christian ages, and we are diminished for it. For God has, in his sovereignty, given us men and women of faith whose lives are examples and whose minds are wellsprings of wisdom and knowledge. If we are to be enriched by them, we must take them up. Indeed, the writer of Hebrews declared that we should bolster our resolve and guard our mission of faith by realizing that a great throng of witnesses, those who have walked the path before us and have been counted faithful, surrounds us.

9. Westminster Confession of Faith, 3.1.

To this end, I commend to you the saints of old. Incorporate them in your time of study. Incorporate them in your time of devotion, in your leisure, in your preaching and teaching. Read the classic texts of Christianity and see if your faith is not strengthened. In God's providence, the classics are invaluable to us. As one Christian author said concerning the classic literature of history:

They guard the truth of the human heart from the faddish half-truths of the day by straightening the mind and imagination and enabling their readers to judge for themselves.[10]

R. C. Sproul, noted theologian and author of over 50 books, declared, "I would gladly have all of the books I have written summarily discarded if the reader would exchange them for the classics."[11]

C. S. Lewis expressed similar sentiments:

Naturally since I am a writer I do not wish the ordinary reader to read no modern books. But if he must read only the new or only the old, I would advise him to read the old.[12]

And though the classic works are not infallible, they can prove indispensable. Or as Lewis states:

Not, of course, that there is any magic about the past. People were no cleverer then than they are now; they made as many

10. Os Guinness and Louise Rowan, eds., *Invitation to the Classics* (Grand Rapids: Baker, 1998), 23.
11. R. C. Sproul, "Take Up and Read Christian Classics," *Tabletalk* (January 1993): 6.
12. C. S. Lewis, *God in the Dock* (Grand Rapids: Eerdmans, 1970), 201.

mistakes as we. But not the same mistakes. They will not flatter us in the errors we are already committing; and their own errors, being now open and palpable, will not endanger us. Two heads are better than one, not because either is infallible but because they are unlikely to go wrong in the same direction.[13]

Clearly, we need not seek out new and novel revelations from God. We simply need to avail ourselves of the faith once and for all delivered to the saints. Indeed, the common heresies so prevalent in our day, for the most part, are not new. They have been asked and answered before. For example:

(1) We need not invent new statements to refute the erroneous teachings of the Jehovah's Witnesses. The church answered their heresy in A.D. 325 when the heresy was known as Arianism. The church unequivocally declared at the Council of Nicaea that according to the Scriptures:

Jesus Christ, the only begotten Son of God, begotten of the Father before all worlds, God of God, Light of Light, Very God of Very God, begotten, not made, being of one substance with the Father.[14]

(2) Though the neo-Pentecostal movement, characterized by the "Toronto Blessing" and "holy laughter," seems to be ever increasing in popularity, we need not grope in the dark for answers to these phenomena. This brand of revivalism that we are witnessing today is not new. Consequently, God has not left us without a witness. In addressing similar revivalism in his day,

13. Ibid., 202.
14. Taken from the Nicene Creed.

Jonathan Edwards, arguably the greatest theologian to grace the American scene, over 250 years ago wrote *Religious Affections*. It remains the seminal work on what are the marks of true revival. He stated:

> [True affections] have their foundation not in self, but in God and Jesus Christ. Therefore, a discovery of themselves and of our own sinfulness will purify their affections; it will not destroy them. In some ways it will sweeten and heighten them. Or to put it another way, *a love of divine things because of the beauty and sweetness of their moral excellence is the beginning and source of all holy affections.*[15]

(3) There has not been a more popular series of books in recent years than Left Behind by Tim LaHaye and Jerry Jenkins, who seem to have tapped into the vein of popular evangelical culture. Yet most seem unaware that the best book ever written illustrating the fate of those who refuse to believe and are subsequently "left behind" was written by a Baptist tinker over three hundred years ago. John Bunyan's *The Pilgrim's Progress* is unparalleled in its historical scope and theological insight. His imagery is biblically based and Christ-centered. Spurgeon, who read *The Pilgrim's Progress* every year of his life, said of Bunyan, "If you were to prick him he would bleed Bible."[16]

(4) Who has set forth a more compelling argument for the design and extent of our Lord's atonement than John Owen in *The Death of Death in the Death of Christ*? For those wrestling with understanding the extent and efficiency of the work of

15. Jonathan Edwards, *Religious Affections*, ed. James Houston (Minneapolis: Bethany House, 1984), 97.
16. Charles Spurgeon, *Pictures from Pilgrim's Progress* (Pasadena, CA: Pilgrim Press, 1992), 6.

Christ, there is no work comparable to that of Owen. J. I. Packer said of Owen's great theological treatise:

> It is safe to say that no comparable exposition of the work of redemption as planned and executed by the triune Jehovah has ever been done since Owen published his. None has been needed . . . no arguments for or against his position have been used since his day, which he has not himself noted and dealt with.[17]

(5) No one has written more eloquently on the doctrine of justification than Horatius Bonar in *The Everlasting Righteousness*. He writes with a sweet familiarity with the divine substitute that is uncommon. Concerning the unfathomable result of justification, Bonar writes:

> So entirely one am I with the sin bearer that God treats me not merely as if I had not done the evil that I have done, but as if I had done all the good which I have not done, but which my substitute had done.[18]

(6) Concerning the oft-discussed subject of free will, Martin Luther's *Bondage of the Will* and Jonathan Edwards's *Freedom of the Will*, hundreds of years after their publication, remain the standards on the subject. To preach and teach on this subject and make no reference to these works is to preach and teach dishonestly. It is to imply that we can uncover and pontificate upon some aspect of this subject that eluded the minds of Luther and Edwards.

17. J. I. Packer, "Introductory Essay," in John Owen, *Death of Death in the Death of Christ* (London: Banner of Truth, 1959), 12–13.
18. Horatius Bonar, *The Everlasting Righteousness* (Hobbs, NM: Trinity Foundation, 1994), 24.

(7) And what of John Calvin's *Institutes of the Christian Religion*? Has there been a more lucid and instructional analysis of the Christian faith? As one professor told me, "All theology since Calvin has been but a postscript for or against Calvin." Any theological library that does not contain the *Institutes* is not a theological library.

This brief excursion into the riches of theological thought contained in the history of Christianity is nowhere near exhaustive. This is just an admonition to avail ourselves of this treasure of gifts that God has in his providence given to us. They are his gifts to us, and we honor him when we enjoy his gifts.

I must confess that I am not a prophet. I have not written to expound some new revelation or novel doctrine. I write not to suggest that God is doing "a new thing." I simply and sincerely commend to you the "faith that was once and for all delivered to the saints." And to this end I say, "Take it up!" We need not—we must not—seek to reinvent Christianity. We simply need to blow the dust off the history of the faith and, as C. S. Lewis said, "allow the clean sea breeze of the centuries to blow through our minds."

We need to "take it up and learn." As African Americans we need to see that this is not only their history; it is our history as well. It is not simply for those who through the years have reconfigured and revised the faces and images of Christianity to look like them. It is our history. We are not simply the sons and daughters of Richard Allen, Absalom Jones, and Andrew Bryan, but we are the sons and daughters of Polycarp, Clement, and Tertullian. We are the sons and daughters of Abraham, Isaac, and Jacob.

So let us "take up and read." As Paul declared in 1 Corinthians 3:21, "For all things are yours." All things are mine. Moses is mine. I can read Genesis and Exodus or I can put it down. It is mine. David is mine. I can read and reflect upon the Psalms at my convenience. Isaiah is mine. Jeremiah, Ezekiel, and all the prophets are mine. Paul, Peter, as well as James and John are mine. But not only that, Augustine and Athanasius are mine. Aquinas and Anselm are mine, too.

Wycliffe is mine. Luther, Calvin, Zwingli, and Knox are mine. Bunyan, Owen, and Baxter are mine. Edwards, Whitefield, and Wesley, along with Newton, Cowper, Watts, and Toplady, are all mine. Spurgeon is mine. Warfield is mine. Dorothy Sayers, Fanny Crosby, Thomas Dorsey are all mine. Campbell-Morgan and Lloyd-Jones are both mine.

J. I. Packer, Machen, Murray, Graham, even MacArthur, Evans, Swindoll, as well as Berkhof, Boice, Piper, Sproul, Horton, Ellis, Nunes, Jones, and all others who name the name of Christ and have demonstrated their commitment to the faith once and for all delivered to the saints—all are mine, and I am Christ's, and Christ is God's.

On Being Black and Reformed: An Interview with Anthony Carter[1]

Why did you write the book *On Being Black and Reformed*?

When I first came into the knowledge of Reformed theology, I was excited and invigorated to share this truth with others. However, I quickly discovered that not everyone found Reformed theology as compelling as I did (go figure). This was particularly true within African-American circles. Because of the caricatures of Reformed theology that have become popular in some Christian circles, and because of the unfortunate history of some within Reformed confessing Christianity, many African Americans find Reformed theology in general, and Reformed-minded Christians in particular, not very sympathetic to their history and culture. I wrote *On Being Black and Reformed* because I wanted to nix those thoughts and demonstrate that

---

1. Parts of the following interview first appeared in the December 2011 issue of *Tabletalk Magazine*. Used with permission.

not only is Reformed theology biblically and historically consistent, but it is not antithetical to the African-American Christian experience. In fact, Reformed theology makes the most sense of the world in general and the history of African Americans in particular.

How did you first discover Reformed theology?

When I was saved and sensed a call to ministry, I set my mind to study the Bible all I could and to learn the teachings contained in there. I had a lot of theological questions and would seek to find answers in a variety of quarters. However, what I discovered was that the vast majority of my answers were coming from guys who held to the Reformed theological tradition. I was not aware of what Reformed theology was at the time, but I knew that the answers I discovered were bathed in the Scriptures.

It was not until I discovered the teachings and writings of J. I. Packer and R.C. Sproul that I began to put the categories together and realized just how mentally compelling, heart-humbling, gospel-centering, and joy-producing Reformed theology could be. Even though I was not surrounded by Reformed-minded Christians and did not attend a Reformed church at the time, the theology was thoroughly convincing and I desired to learn all I could.

A number of American Reformed theologians were slave owners. How can a Christian who is black embrace the theology of men who owned slaves or who defended the slave trade?

Indeed, this is one of the hurdles that many (not all) African-American Christians find hard to get over as they come to understand and embrace Reformed theology. I have often contended that the reticence that some African Americans have toward an embrace of Reformed theology is not due as much to the theology as it is to the ones who have held to it. There are, however, a couple things to be said about this.

First, the sordid, sinful, and tangled history of slavery in America was not just the property of Reformed Christians. Christians from practically every religious confession in America have a poor history of racism and even slave holding. To disregard any tradition that held slaves would be to disregard practically every theological tradition in America. Secondly, while other traditions have been quicker to acknowledge their sins in this regard, many in the Reformed tradition have been slow to and have even retreated into their own theological and cultural enclaves rather than deal publicly and forthrightly with the transgressions of the past. Consequently, Reformed Christians have been viewed as less vigorous in denouncing the sins of slavery, thus implying their approval of it. This perception is unfortunate, yet real.

Nevertheless, the question remains. To answer it, allow me to make it personal. How can I, a black man, embrace the theology of men who owned slaves? I can joyfully embrace it because I realize that I am embracing the theology of the Bible and not necessarily the frail, fallible men who teach it. I can embrace the theology because it allows me to point out the sins of such teachers and yet the grace that is greater than that sin.

How could the early Christians embrace the theology of the apostle Paul when, as Saul of Tarsus, he pursued and persecuted them and even consented to many of their deaths? They could do it because they understood the gospel to be greater than not just their sins but also the sins of those who transgressed against them. Obviously, Paul repented of the sins he had perpetrated against the church prior to knowing the Lord, and he sought to do all he could to make up for his error. Nevertheless, we should never assume that it was easy for him to live down his transgressions against the church. And knowing human nature, no doubt

149

some Christians struggled to receive Paul knowing his history (we tend to be less forgiving than we think). Consequently, I can embrace it because if we listen and learn only from those in history who have no theological blind spots, then to whom shall we listen and from whom shall we learn? Biblical theology must be larger, even grander than the imperfections of its teachers. I believe Reformed theology is.

What is your opinion regarding the largely non-integrated state of local churches?

For years, the evangelical church has decried the ethnic and cultural divide that is found in local churches. While we are comfortable with and even insistent upon integration in larger society, for some reason we have not been able to achieve integration within the walls of our local churches. God has given us a vision for it in the Scriptures and even in our hearts, but, apparently, he has not allowed that vision to come to full fruition in the vast majority of our congregations. The fact that the church is not the most integrated institution in society is troublesome when you consider that we have the one message and power to bring about true reconciliation, namely, the gospel and the Holy Spirit. Nevertheless, I do understand the difficulty.

Most of us like comfort. We like to be around people with whom we are comfortable and have much in common. This is particularly true when it comes to those places that mean the most to us—home and church. Thus, not only are our churches not integrated, but even more rarely are our families integrated.

Still, this lack of integration is not something with which we should be comfortable. The vision of the Scriptures is clear. The vision in most of our minds is clear (I don't know too many people who don't want to see their churches more integrated). The question to consider is whether our churches are places where people sense that Christ is celebrated—not culture, class, or ethnicity, but Christ. It is difficult not to celebrate culture, class, and ethnicity. Yet this is what we are called to do. This is what we are called to strive after. The fact that our churches are not integrated is not as troublesome for me as the fact that culture and ethnicity often trump the gospel, even in what we might believe to be the best of churches.

How is being black and reformed different today than it was when you wrote *On Being Black and Reformed* thirteen years ago? What does the future look like?

When I sat down and began writing *On Being Black and Reformed*, I was not aware of many vocal and openly confessing black and Reformed preachers and teachers. There is no doubt that they were there and serving faithfully in the places where God had called them, but I was only aware of a few. Today, there is a growing, confident, and engaged community of black and Reformed voices throughout Christianity, and I could not be more excited. From the pulpit, to the seminary, to music, the arts, the classroom, the mission field, politics, and beyond, you will find black men and women who openly profess the Reformed faith. In fact, the resurgence and popularity of Christian hip-hop today is largely due to the influence and gifts of Reformed-minded artists. Also, the Internet has become an indispensable medium for connecting and providing unparalleled opportunities to better understand and communicate the faith we profess. Today, conferences are being lead, networks developed, and churches planted by the young, black, and Reformed. The young, black, and Reformed can be found in a variety of places on the Internet giving articulate theological voice to the major issues of our day. In fact, Reformed black voices have been leading the way in challenging the greater

Reformed community in understanding ideas of social justice and human dignity today.

Race has once again become a topic of conversation in the general public with cases of police brutality targeted at black men and women, and church shootings and bombings by supposed racist individuals. What, if anything, does Reformed theology have to say to these issues?

When we think of the Reformation, we often only think of it as a theological movement. It was definitely that. The recovering of the gospel—in particular, the doctrine of justification by faith alone—was at the core of the Reformation, and without it the Reformation would not have been what it was. However, the Reformation was more than just a theological movement. It was also a movement of social justice, recovering once again a biblical emphasis on individual human dignity and the *imago dei* (image of God) in everyone.

Issues of racism and social injustice are largely rooted in a lack of respect for and understanding the inherent dignity granted by God to each man and woman he has created. Even though we are all born sinners and our wills are by nature enslaved to sin, there remains in each of us the image of God, which cries out for respect. When disrespected or denied this inherent dignity, men and women eventually rebel, and violence and loss of life is frequently the unfortunate result. Through the years, Reformed theology has articulated as well as any the importance of the image of God, the dignity of his creation, and the importance of understanding these in how we relate to each other. Unfortunately, there have been times in the history of the church where Reformed voices have not emphasized these teachings, particularly when the treatment or mistreatment of minorities or the disenfranchised is concerned. However, one of

152

the beauties of Reformed theology is its holistic approach. All of life belongs to God. As Reformed theologian and statesman Abraham Kuyper famously said, "There is not a square inch in the whole domain of our human existence over which Christ, who is sovereign over all, does not cry, 'Mine!'" This includes the dignity of all people and how we treat those who seem to be different from us. When those in authority see that all people have dignity and worth because they are made in the image of God, there will be fewer and fewer unfortunate deaths. Reformed theology teaches that everyone is on the same level ground before God—that is, a sinner in need of a Savior.

In the aftermath of the horrific murder of nine black people at Emanuel African Methodist Episcopal Church during prayer and Bible study on June of 2015, many wondered how the church would respond to the hateful rage of the young white supremacist who perpetrated the act. Unsurprisingly, the victims' family and the church responded with the love and forgiveness of Christ. Even while grieving the senseless loss of loved ones and seeking answers to almost unanswerable questions, the church and many of the families offered the love of Christ in return.

Because the church has been the symbol of black independence in America and the bulwark of hope, the black church has frequently been the target of hate-filled, racist-motivated attacks. She has endured bombings, burnings, gunmen, and more. And yet her indomitable spirit still presses on because of her history and trust in a sovereign God.

The history of the black church in the United States has been a history of leaning upon the sovereign love of God. This has not only caused black Christians to find hope in midst of seemingly hopeless situations, but it has also allowed black Christians to forgive the seemingly unforgivable. The black church, as an institution, for all her faults, is arguably the most loving, welcoming, and forgiving institution in the world. Sovereign love has been the theme of the black church in America. Sovereign love is at the heart of Reformed theology. It is why I love both and seek to bring them together.

If you could study under any theologian in church history (excluding those in Scripture), who would it be and why?

Having attended Reformed Theological Seminary in Orlando, and having worked at Ligonier for five years, I have had the unbelievable blessing of being exposed to and taught by some great theologians. And so, if I exclude not only the men given to us in the Scriptures (e.g., Paul, Peter, etc.), but also, with respect, men like R.C. Sproul and Richard Pratt, from whom I have learned as much if not more than anyone, I would say that I would be most excited to study under Wilhelmus à Brakel (1635–1711). Admittedly, most would not be familiar with à Brakel and his theological magnum opus, *The Christian's Reasonable Service*, but I have never been so moved by theological reflection as I am with à Brakel's. À Brakel had the unique ability to take heady theological reflection and make it not just pastoral, but even emotion stirring. Coming from the rich Dutch Reformed tradition, his biblical theological reflections are keen, but he never settles just for keenness. His goal seems to be experiential—a rich, Reformed, experiential Christianity. That's what I pray to have.

Having spent countless hours poring over à Brakel, I feel in some sense that I have studied under him. However, what a joy it would have been to be an eyewitness to the effect his theological insights had on his heart and the hearts of those to whom he was called to minister. Wilhelmus à Brakel was not black, but when I read him I get the sense that his preaching would have been right at home in any black and Reformed church I know.

Recommended Reading

AFRICAN-AMERICAN CHRISTIANITY

Anyabwile, Thabiti. *The Decline of African-American Theology: From Biblical Faith to Cultural Captivity.* Downers Grove, IL: Intervarsity Academic Press, 2007.

———. *The Faithful Preacher: Recapturing the Vision of Three Pioneering African-American Pastors.* Wheaton, IL: Crossway Books, 2007.

———. *May We Meet in the Heavenly World: The Piety of Lemuel Haynes.* Grand Rapids: Reformation Heritage Books, 2009.

———. *Reviving the Black Church: New Life for a Sacred Institution.* Nashville: B&H Books, 2015.

Bradley, Anthony. *Liberating Black Theology: The Bible and the Black Experience in America.* Wheaton, IL: Crossway Books, 2010.

Carter, Anthony J., ed. *Experiencing the Truth: Bringing the Reformation to the African-American Church.* Wheaton, IL: Crossway Books, 2008.

———. *Glory Road: The Journeys of 10 African-Americans into Reformed Christianity.* Wheaton, IL: Crossway Books, 2009.

Ellis, Carl F., Jr. *Free at Last?* Downers Grove, IL: InterVarsity Press, 1996.

Evans, Tony. *Let's Get to Know Each Other.* Nashville: Nelson, 1995.

Fields, Bruce. *Introducing Black Theology.* Grand Rapids: Baker, 2001.

Fitts, Leroy. *A History of Black Baptists*. Nashville: Broadman, 1985.

Hatch, Nathan. *The Democratization of American Christianity*. New Haven, CT: Yale University Press, 1989.

Keener, Craig and Glenn Usry. *Black Man's Religion*. Downers Grove, IL: InterVarsity Press, 1996.

————. *Defending Black Faith*. Downers Grove, IL: InterVarsity Press, 1997.

Lincoln, C. Eric and Lawrence H. Mamiya. *The Black Church in the African American Experience*. Durham, NC: Duke University Press, 1990.

Perry, Dwight. *Breaking Down Barriers*. Grand Rapids: Baker, 1998.

Raboteau, Albert. *Slave Religion: The Invisible Institution in the Antebellum South*. New York: Oxford University Press, 1978.

Saillant, John. *Black Puritan, Black Republican: The Life and Thought of Lemuel Haynes (1753–1833)*. New York: Oxford Press, 2003.

Warren, Gwendolyn Sims. *Ev'ry Time I Feel the Spirit*. New York: Henry Holt and Company, 1997.

Washington, James M. *Conversations with God*. New York: Harper Perennial, 1995.

Williams, Harry Louis, II. *No Easy Walk*. Downers Grove, IL: InterVarsity Press, 1998.

Williams, Juan, and Quinton Dixie. *This Far by Faith*. New York: Harper Collins, 2003.

REFORMED THEOLOGY

Baptist Confession of 1689 (London Confession).

Berkhof, Louis. *Systematic Theology*. Grand Rapids: Eerdmans, 1939.

Boettner, Loraine. *Reformed Doctrine of Predestination*. Phillipsburg, NJ: Presbyterian and Reformed, 1963.

Calvin, John. *Institutes of the Christian Religion*. 2 vols. Translated by Ford L. Battles. Edited by John T. McNeill. Grand Rapids: Eerdmans, 1989.

Clark, Erskine. *Our Southern Zion: The History of Calvinism in the South Carolina Low Country, 1690-1990*. Tuscaloosa, AL: University of Alabama Press, 1996.

Cosby, Brian. *Rebels Rescued: A Student's Guide to Reformed Theology*. Scotland: Christian Focus Publications, 2012.

Foster, Greg. *The Joy of Calvinism: Knowing God's Personal, Unconditional, Irresistible, Unbreakable Love*. Wheaton, IL: Crossway Books, 2012.

Grudem, Wayne. *Systematic Theology*. Grand Rapids: Zondervan, 1994.

Hagopian, David, ed. *Back to Basics*. Phillipsburg, NJ: P&R Publishing, 1996.

Hodge, Charles. *Systematic Theology*. 3 vols. Grand Rapids: Eerdmans, 1960.

Horton, Michael. *Putting Amazing Back in Grace*. Grand Rapids: Baker, 1991.

Owen, John. *The Death of Death in the Death of Christ*. London: Banner of Truth, 1959.

Packer, J. I. *Evangelism and the Sovereignty of God*. Downers Grove, IL: InterVarsity Press, 1991.

———. *Knowing God*. Downers Grove, IL: InterVarsity Press, 1973.

Pink, Arthur. *The Sovereignty of God*. London: Banner of Truth, 1961.

Piper, John. *The Pleasures of God*. Rev. ed. Sisters, OR: Multnomah, 2000.

Schreiner, Thomas and Bruce Ware, eds. *Grace of God and the Bondage of the Will*. Grand Rapids: Baker, 1995.

Sproul, R. C. *Grace Unknown*. Grand Rapids: Baker, 1997.

Steele, David N. and Curtis C. Thomas. *The Five Points of Calvinism*. Phillipsburg, NJ: Presbyterian and Reformed, 1963.

Wells, David, ed. *Reformed Theology in America*. Grand Rapids: Baker, 1997.

Westminster Confession of Faith.

White, James R. *Potter's Freedom*. Amityville, NY: Calvary Press Reformed Publishing, 2000.

Williams, Jarvis. *For Whom Did Christ Die? The Extent of the Atonement in Paul's Theology*. Milton Keynes, UK: Paternoster Publishing, 2012.